SEXUALITY MENTALITY

Creating a Culture of Biblical Integrity

HEATHER RUESCH

CONCORDIA PUBLISHING HOUSE · SAINT LOUIS

Sexuality Mentality

CREATING A CULTURE OF BIBLICAL INTEGRITY

HEATHER RUESCH

CONCORDIA PUBLISHING HOUSE • SAINT LOUIS

Concordia
Publishing House

Published by Concordia Publishing House

3558 S. Jefferson Ave., St. Louis, MO 63118-3968

1-800-325-3040 • www.cph.org

Manufactured in the United States of America

LIBRARY OF CONGRESS CATALOGING-IN-PUBLICATION DATA
Names: Ruesch, Heather, author.
Title: Sexuality mentality : creating a culture of biblical integrity /
Heather Ruesch.
Description: Saint Louis, MO : Concordia Publishing House, [2018] | Includes
bibliographical references.
Identifiers: LCCN 2018019461 (print) | LCCN 2018032275 (ebook) | ISBN
9780758659927 | ISBN 9780758659910
Subjects: LCSH: Sex--Religious aspects--Christianity.
Classification: LCC BT708 (ebook) | LCC BT708 .R845 2018 (print) | DDC
241/.664--dc23
LC record available at https://lccn.loc.gov/2018019461

---

1 2 3 4 5 6 7 8 9 10   27 26 25 24 23 22 21 20 19 18

Dedication

One day, a long time ago, my husband bought me the foundational part of this book—my own study Bible. When I opened the front cover, he had written the following:

Honey, some things you read in the Bible leave you asking questions. I think this will help you answer a lot of them.

I have certainly had many questions about my faith and why we, as Christians, believe what we do about life, family, love, sacrifice, and forgiveness. God's Word has never let me down. Thank you, Matt, for always feeding my soul with this good spiritual food and encouraging me with it daily. Having you, Bella, Paul, and Sofia by my side is the greatest honor of my life and made writing this book all the more special. I thank God every day that I get to call you . . .

my family.

Table of Contents

Foreword - - - - - - - - - - - - - - - - - 15

Introduction - - - - - - - - - - - - - - - 19

Chapter 1: Propaganda - - - - - - - - - - - - 25

The Hot Stove 25
Pulling a Madison Avenue 27
It's Too Important 30
The Twenty-Five-Cent Bouncy Ball 31
The Simple Things in Life 33
It's a Frame of Mind 37
Chapter 1 Discussion Questions 42

Chapter 2: There's No Such Thing as Safe Sex - - - - - - 45
(Outside of Marriage)

The Trouble with Condoms and Birth Control 47
More Than Just a Physical Body 56
Physical Consequences of Sex outside of Marriage 57
Unplanned Pregnancy 58
Sexually Transmitted Infections and Diseases 63
The Rest of Me: Mental, Emotional, Social, and Spiritual 72
Chapter 2 Discussion Questions 74

Chapter 3: Pornography, Modesty, - - - - - - - - 77
and Sexual Propaganda

The Mentality of the Body 77
Self-Esteem: Knowing Your Value 82
Modesty 84
Pornography and Self-Pleasure 89
The Link between Sexual Harassment and Pornography 93
Pornography and Marriage 97
Machismo 99
Chapter 3 Discussion Questions 102

Chapter 4: Teens and Homosexuality - - - - - - - - -105

Communication   108
Identifying as LGBTQIA   109
The Identity of the Family   112
The Bible, Our Operations Manual   117
Coexisting   121
Being Courteous Never Gets Old   122
Chapter 4 Discussion Questions   126

Chapter 5: What Is True Love? - - - - - - - - - -129

What Does True Love Look Like?   133
The Dangling Carrot   137
Chapter 5 Discussion Questions   140

Chapter 6: Christian Dating - - - - - - - - - - -143

The General Operating System   143
The Mission Statement   146
The Standards of Procedure   149
The Line in the Sand   152
The Moment of Truth about Temptation   154
Chapter 6 Discussion Questions   158

Chapter 7: Starting Over - - - - - - - - - - - 161

Chapter 7 Discussion Questions   168

Foreword

We are in a battle! If you are a parent, a grandparent, a youth leader or pastor, or just someone who cares deeply about teens, then you are well aware of the battle being waged against this generation. The battle is not "us," the big adults, against "them," the vulnerable teens; the battle is against an enemy that has been waging war against humankind from the beginning. As Paul described to the believers in Ephesus, "For we do not wrestle against flesh and blood, but against the rulers, against the authorities, against the cosmic powers over this present darkness, against the spiritual forces of evil in the heavenly places" (Ephesians 6:12).

Peter describes the enemy this way: "Be sober-minded; be watchful. Your adversary the devil prowls around like a roaring lion, seeking someone to devour" (1 Peter 5:8).

When that lion roars loudly and the battle rages, it is tempting to run and hide, wave a white flag of surrender, or crumble in defeat. Please don't! Arm yourselves with knowledge, train yourself with good teaching, gird your loins with truth, take up your sword and fight!

In a culture that insinuates that parents are powerless and communicates that as a parent your values and input are meaningless and will have no impact, you need to hear the voice of truth. The truth is, Mom and Dad, YOU MATTER! And your voice is far more powerful than the culture, peers, and the media! In every single study done on youth behavior and risk assessment, the most influential voice for teens is their parents. The others aren't even close. This is why you must use your voice. You must communicate your values, and communicate them OFTEN (the eye roll with "you've told me a million times" was always my payday!). If you are a parent of a teen, or a grandparent even, please heed every word on the pages ahead of you.

You hold in your hands an amazing tool—a battle plan filled with truth, with instruction, with clear marching orders. My friend Heather Ruesch has so beautifully written about the battle for the hearts and minds of our children and about the necessity for family and community to come alongside them in a powerful way that shines a bright light into the darkness. Heather speaks as a fellow soldier, as one who has fought for her own life, for her precious children, and for the many teens God has called her to reach. Her love for Jesus, for her family, and for the Body of Christ is evident on each page.

I pray that you will not simply read this amazing book, but that you will put into practice the wisdom it contains. I pray that you will share this with fellow soldiers in the battle in your community and that you will hear the battle cry and not shrink in fear, but stand firm in your convictions. Your teens' very souls depend upon it!

"Therefore take up the whole armor of God, that you may be able to withstand in the evil day, and having done all, to stand firm" (Ephesians 6:13).

Onward!

Pam Stenzel, MA
Founder, Enlighten Communications
Senior Regional Clinic Director, Community Pregnancy Clinics, Inc.

Introduction

In the spring of 2012, I had been serving as the executive director of a crisis pregnancy center in central Wisconsin for a little over a year. My husband was settled in as the pastor of two beautiful Lutheran churches there, and our kids were fully immersed in classes at the Lutheran school close by. Because I worked in pro-life ministry, I was regularly approached with questions about pregnancy, planned and unplanned, and of course abortion and life issues as well. I loved every minute of it then; I still do.

One afternoon as I was picking up my kids from school, a mom flagged me down and asked if I could recommend any Christian materials for youth pertaining to sex education. Surprisingly, I hadn't spent a lot of time on this aspect of life-issues ministry, but it made sense for me to look into it. I didn't have a lot of information for her that day, but I promised to get back to her soon. I assumed that the Christian schools in our area would have some kind of curriculum they were using, so I started calling around. You guys, none of them were teaching a sexual integrity curriculum or an organized Human Growth and Development curriculum. None of them. I inquired of the Christian schools outside our area—same thing. Everyone I spoke with expressed the need for such a program, but for many complicated and legitimate reasons, they just didn't even know where to begin.

That's when my passion began for teaching sexual integrity to youth. From a very young age, I remember having a strong conviction to be a good mom and have a great marriage. I know I'm not the only one. Little kids, girls and boys, all over the world have spent the foundational parts of their lives rocking baby dolls and making dinner for their play families in their preschool kitchens. The topic of how quickly kids grow up regularly came up on coffee klatch mornings with other parents and in adult Bible studies on Sunday. We all knew that we had to do better. How were our children and society's children going to stand a chance of having a healthy family life someday? After we lamented the direction things were going, though, we would maybe say a prayer and then continue with other discussions. No resolutions. No plan of attack. Just sympathy. I worked in life-issues ministry, for Pete's sake, and I was just as guilty!

Through the prompting of the beautiful mama who approached me that day, I was given the opportunity to focus a moment of my life intentionally on the prevention of cultural ignorance about God's intentions for sex, relationships, and the human body. That conversation in the school parking lot led to the development of our pregnancy center's Emberlife Teens for Life Program. I was trained through the Abstinence and Marriage Partnership in Chicago to teach the Excel Abstinence Education curriculum, and together with four other young adults from our local center, I began taking the curriculum into the local churches and Christian schools. Over the course of a couple of years, that message of hope for youth took off, and I began speaking all across the country. Because I had experience as a life-issues speaker and singer/songwriter for five years prior to serving at the pregnancy center, I was used to being in front of other people; however, this ministry brought with it a whole new challenge. So many people have trouble talking about sex with their closest friends or even their spouses. How was I going to speak about these things with youth? Especially youth who aren't my own?

But I was convicted. I saw an area of tremendous need that I couldn't ignore. I kept thinking, "They don't know. Our kids are having to wing it out there because they don't know. We have not equipped them." I began studying and paying more attention to the youth we served at the Center, in our churches, and everywhere else I went. I began gathering every resource I could find about God's intentions for sex and relationships. I wanted to talk to these girls (and the boys as well) *before* they reached the point of making ill-informed decisions. As a pregnancy center director, I basically wanted to put myself out of work. It is always the goal of pro-life ministry workers to strive for a world that advocates for God's value of human life so much that our services are no longer necessary. Admittedly, this frame of mind is pie-in-the-sky because of our sinful, fallen world. Nonetheless, we approach every day with that goal in mind and continue on, encouraged by our Lord who goes with us and never fails us.

I imagine that many of you who are reading right now feel the same way. You know that it's essential that we speak clearly and boldly to our youth, who are being bombarded by mainstream culture. You know that there needs to be a voice that counters the world's message of "Listen to your heart," "Do what feels good," and "Baby, you were born this way." God has designed sex to be a precious gift to be enjoyed—when it's according to His design.

I wanted to write this book to unify us all with a clear

and direct understanding of God's intentions for sex and relationships. As we gain confidence to speak with integrity on this topic, in all its forms, we encourage others to do the same. And the momentum builds. We, as members of the Body of Christ, gain strength and power in numbers as we unite around true teaching and doctrine. *And lives will change.*

Each chapter is designed to expound on the previous to continue that momentum. I hope to connect the dots for you, so to speak, to help you recall with ease ways to address the important concepts that we all wish we had on the tip of our tongues. This book focuses, primarily, on relationship and emotional intelligence in regard to our youth and our families and what it means to live with biblical sexual integrity.

Additionally, I've included a short recap in the form of questions at the end of every chapter to help those concepts really sink in and to make it easy to incorporate this book into a Bible study, book club, or other small group setting. Therefore, I encourage you to use this book as a jumping-off point to dig deeper. Start here. Use the many talking points contained within to open up some discussion with the teenagers in your life. Every topic I've ever encountered while working in youth ministry is touched on in this book and freely given to assist you in whatever ways you need them.

- The value of human life
- Casual sex
- Unplanned pregnancy
- Contraceptives
- Pornography
- Self-pleasure
- Homosexuality
- Sexual harassment
- Sexual abuse
- Modesty and self-esteem

- True love
- Christian dating
- Preparing your kids for temptation
- The value of marriage
- How to parent for biblical sexual integrity

This is a daunting task, but we can do it. We *must* do it. We must find our voice on these issues and fulfill the calling that God has given us as parents, pastors, teachers, youth workers, and those who care about teens. As I share my experiences of communicating God's gift and design of sex to youth, I pray that this book will help you to find your own voice as well!

Joyfully,

Heather

CHAPTER 1

Propaganda

Your tongue plots destruction,
    like a sharp razor, you worker of deceit.
You love evil more than good,
    and lying more than speaking what is right.
You love all words that devour,
    O deceitful tongue.

PSALM 52:2–5

THE HOT STOVE

I have three beautiful kids. They are my pride and joy. A great many of the lessons I've learned about life and integrity, I've learned from or because of them. Humbling thought, isn't it? That God would use these vulnerable little people as the means to deliver such vast insights and wisdom to us? I love that.

I remember one time when my son was just a toddler. I was in the kitchen cooking noodles, and he did what many curious (and ninja-like) little kids do: he reached up to touch the hot stove. After bandaging his tiny fingers and snuggling him close, I was overwhelmed with guilt. Why hadn't I seen that coming? If only I'd moved faster. If only

I had taught him beforehand that the stove was hot, he wouldn't have gotten burned. I vowed from that moment on that I would always catch my children before they hurt themselves, for the rest of their lives!

Well, we all know that no such vow could be kept. There is absolutely no way I could ever achieve such an ambitious goal, no matter how well-intended it was. My children, all three of them, went on to scrape knees, break toes, and much more for years to come. What I did learn from that incident, however, is that I wasn't powerless. God gave me, the parent, the authority and the wisdom to teach my children. Through intentionality and instruction, simply by making it a priority to teach safety in our home, I could help them discern the difference between what would be good for them and what would be harmful. Instead of being filled with guilt, watching them go through painful situations and wishing I had done something sooner, I began equipping them with the tools and knowledge they needed to mini-mize the danger around them and, ultimately, the effects of that danger in their lives.

It's proved to be a far better approach in the end, and I'm happy to report that no one else in our family has been burned by the stove since!

How many of us, if we saw a child reaching for a hot stove, would stop him or her immediately? We, as adults, through our experiences, know that the stove is hot and unquestionably would cause pain and injury to the child. Yet I've listened as so many parents over the years have said things such as this: "It's unrealistic, in this day and age, for me to expect that my child won't have sex before he gets married." Or "I'm just glad they're being safe," as if to imply that sex outside of marriage is somehow safer when using birth control or condoms. I'll get into that topic more in chapter 2, but I contend that this mentality among us is the equivalent of watching a child approach the stove, reach for it, and nod in approval as he burns himself.

Now, I know that the vast majority of us are not actively seeking ways to hurt our kids—that's ridiculous. We love our kids, and we want what's best for them. The problem is this: We've been had. Tricked. Duped. And we didn't even see it coming. Sure, there have been some cultural movements over the years that certainly didn't sit well with us as Christians: the legalization of abortion, the campaigns boosting casual sex, the unleashing of the homosexual lifestyle, and the divorce rate among American families. We absolutely saw those trends and we dejectedly registered them in our mental file cabinet, unsure how to prevent them or even how to confront them.

What I'm delving into, though, is what precedes all of that: the conversations (or lack thereof) between people and the knowledge (or lack thereof) contained in those conversations that were the driving force behind these movements. This was where the lie gained momentum. This was where the church grew too casual about defending every human life with the veracity it deserves. It's ironic that this war on life may be happening in part, albeit unintentionally, because of our leadership during the past several decades.

This was the moment when we watched our children touch the stove.

PULLING A MADISON AVENUE

We live in a culture that has perfected the art of distraction. This past summer, our family visited the Holocaust Museum in Orlando, Florida, where we listened, watched, and mourned over the tragic loss of lives under the reign of German ruler Adolf Hitler. As an extension of the museum, there is an exhibit highlighting the effects of marketing propaganda throughout the twentieth and twenty-first centuries. To be clear, propaganda is biased information that is designed to shape public opinion and behavior. A major advantage that allowed Hitler and his army to eliminate almost an entire demographic of human beings, approximately six million people of Jewish heritage and faith, was the targeted marketing and propaganda against them that took place over several years leading up to the Holocaust. The German Nazi regime intentionally zeroed in on them, convinced people they were an inferior yet threatening race, and then plotted to murder them all. The population of Germany that wasn't Jewish or Nazi—the majority of whom were good, honest, faithful people—supported these horrific events because, well, they'd "been had," just like us, through means of biased propaganda. This propaganda created superficial convictions that never developed into more extensive thinking about the value of human life.

Here at home, I'm reminded of those well-oiled machines working on Madison Avenue (the advertising and marketing capital of the United States) since the 1920s. The term *Madison Avenue* has become a shortcut to refer to the gimmicky, slick use of the communications media to play on people's emotions.

These agencies have been targeting specific demographics, focusing on race, age, gender, religion, salary, and more, for the better part of ninety years. For nearly a century, there have been people whose only job, forty-plus hours a

week, has been to study the public and feed us what their
clients want us to know in the way we are most likely to
receive it.

> Modern propaganda draws upon techniques and strategies
> used in advertising, public relations, communications, and
> mass psychology. It simplifies complicated issues or ideology
> for popular consumption, is always biased, and is geared to
> achieving a particular end. Propaganda generally employs
> symbols, whether in written, musical, or visual forms, and
> plays upon and channels complex human emotions towards a
> desired goal. It is often employed by governmental and private
> organizations to promote their causes and institutions and
> denigrate their opponents. Propaganda functions as just one
> weapon in the arsenal of mass persuasion.
>
> In contrast to the ideal of an educator, who aims to foster
> independent judgment and thinking, the practitioner of pro-
> paganda does not aim to encourage deliberation by present-
> ing a variety of viewpoints and leaving it up to the audience
> to determine which perspective is correct. The propagandist
> transmits only information geared to strengthen his or her case,
> and consciously omits detrimental information.
>
> Not all propaganda is bad. Propaganda is used to shape
> opinion and behavior. . . . The real danger of propaganda lies
> when competing voices are silenced—and unchecked, propa-
> ganda can have negative consequences.
>
> **—UNITED STATES HOLOCAUST MEMORIAL MUSEUM**[1]

Did you get that? The job of the propagandist is to spin a
concept or a product, for his paying client, in a way that will

---

1   Resources, "What Is Propaganda?" United States Holocaust Memorial Museum,
     https://www.ushmm.org/propaganda/resources/ (accessed April 23, 2018).

make the consumer want to buy or endorse it. Just off the top of my head, I can think of countless deplorable ways I've seen sexual propaganda at work in the lives of our children and our families.

Additionally, this illustration puts into words what most Christians are feeling in our culture today: Everything in the media about sexuality and the value of human life is one-sided. The logic is missing. The depth is missing. The morality is missing. Without a doubt, Satan has his hands all over this.

If this all sounds a little bit crazy, that's because it absolutely is. It's crazy that so much of what really matters in the world has been shifted down in priority to make room for consumerism: a designer kitchen, dream family vacations, new cars, and cute outfits. I love a beautiful, fall-themed harvest party complete with mini pumpkins and chai lattes as much as the next girl, but the minute said party becomes a distraction from instructing my children in the faith and keeping our family unit focused on God's will for our lives, I need to throw it away. I don't have time for that. I'm fighting every day to keep my family's eyes on the things of God and not on the things of this world.

IT'S TOO IMPORTANT

At first glimpse, working hard to have nice things isn't bad. Enjoying nice things isn't bad. Don't misinterpret what I'm saying here. I highly respect all working parents who are providing for their families. The breakdown happens when the little things become the priority and the big things are just too much to deal with today.

We put them off until tomorrow.

Hey, there's a teacher willing to teach my child about sex? Whew! Great.

Check that off the list of big things to do and try to knock out the next one. I've been there. It's like trying to juggle snow cones. Everything feels urgent, all the time.

As a mom, but also as a girl who was pregnant and contemplating abortion at the age of nineteen, I can tell you with confidence that teaching sexual integrity to your kids is not something you want to hand over to just anybody.

It's too important.

The irrevocable value of human life is the foundation on which every other critical decision they will ever face is built. It is this foundation that establishes how we regard one another sexually as well.

THE TWENTY-FIVE-CENT BOUNCY BALL

As Christians, we wonder how our world has gotten so twisted. Whatever is good, sound, and just has been exchanged for that which is demented, destructive, and superficial. Why is this? Because sex and vanity sell. They sell because so many have bought into this idea that quantity is better than quality. The value of human life is actively being defaced.

The irony of it all is that the people pushing this agenda in the entertainment and advertising industries are the ones who are suffering the most. They can't see that they are more valuable than all the money and beauty in the world. They don't know this Savior, Jesus, who suffered and bore all their hurts and imperfections that they might have a life full of the purest love humanity can ever know. As Christians and imitators of Christ, we are called to approach even untrustworthy people with love.

What happened to them? What life experiences led them to the places they are now, stuffing themselves like gluttons with superficial, momentary highs of money and power and lust, only to move on to the next big thing, hoping that this time it will be different, more satisfying, complete? These struggling people have my heart.

They have my heart because I am just like them. I *am* them, except for one world-changing difference: I know my sin, and I confess it. As I confess it, I am cleansed of it. And as I am cleansed of it, I strive to refine and realign my thoughts and actions with the Word of God. It's a daily, sometimes minute-by-minute, cycle that I will continue to wash, rinse, and repeat for the rest of my life.

SCRIPTURE CONNECTION

For the LORD your God is gracious and merciful and will not turn away His face from you, if you return to Him. (2 Chronicles 30:9)

It occurred to me early in my pro-life work that if I've been able to discern this complex and intentional underpinning of the marketing industry only after about ten years of my ministry, then the odds looked pretty good for those prowlers out there who have been profiting from people's weaknesses for a century now. They've really had time to hone their craft. The reality is that our vulnerabilities put money in the pockets of those whose lives revolve around superficial highs. That right there is the motivation and the momentum that keeps this monster fed. Vulnerabilities such as addiction, neglect, and the human desire for love at all costs. Not to mention the actual monster behind it all: Satan. He is the orchestrator of all evil. His influence and string-pulling in the entertainment and advertising industry is calculated and deliberate.

Right under our noses, with our consent by omission, the media and our culture are allowed to portray sex and human life as something no more valuable than the twenty-five-cent bouncy ball in the grocery store checkout line: fun to play with (until it's not anymore) and easily replaced.

The gift of your entire body, soul, and mind—for which the Son of God has died—in the most intimate and personal bond you could ever share with another living being has been perverted into a fleeting and superficial satisfaction of the carnal appetite.

The most tragic exploit is that the world would have us believe that this is *it*. That this is as deep and as real as it gets. Our youth are searching for real love, the kind of love that fills us with peace, hope, and strength to face the day. The kind of love where you know you belong. And yet, today hopelessness consumes so many of our youth instead.

The reality is that by our absence from the global conversation, we as Christians, as parents and families and workers in the Church, endorse what the culture is selling. Propaganda has filled our minds, and we've begun to see "love" as the world sees it, rather than seeing it how God sees it: as love that does no wrong to its neighbor (Romans 13:10).

THE SIMPLE THINGS IN LIFE

Little House on the Prairie was one of my favorite television shows when I was a kid. (I read all the books too.) I think we should be striving to live more like the Ingalls family. I get groans and giggles every time I say that in a public place, but hear me out. About three years ago, I made the decision to approach my life with a new mentality, a new mission statement, so to speak:

Simplify.

Simplify it all, and spend a year bringing every aspect of life that stressed me out back to that action word.

What were the things that were stressing me out? I felt as if my kids were growing more distant and our family was becoming disjointed. My husband seemed irritated with me. A lot. My home was always cluttered. We never seemed to have enough money. I was overweight.

All of these stressors took on a new meaning when I suddenly had a solution I could apply to them: simplify. Instead of running all around town, taking kids to any number of places or events, we stayed home and hung out together whenever possible. By simplifying our schedules and the way we ate, we saved a lot of money and began to lose weight too! It turns out that my husband was irritated with me mostly because I was irritated with myself and how complicated our lives had become. It's going on four years, and the simplicity mind-set is still going strong at our house! Although not without tenderly caring for it and keeping it a priority. It's hard work that makes the rest of our lives easier.

Consumerism has infiltrated the American family so deeply. An incredibly significant part of the consumer culture is the emphasis on material goods and lifestyle as the keys to happiness and satisfaction. It's the classic "keeping up with the Joneses" mentality. Our family, like so many

others, had fallen into the belief that a new gadget, member-
ship, or product was magically going to improve our quality
of life.

Do you see how, as a culture of people, we've allowed
stuff to consume us? I wonder if that's why it's called *consumerism*. Madison Avenue has achieved what it set out to
do: to make us want their products more than anything else
in this world.

Living like the Ingalls family is looking pretty good all of
a sudden, isn't it? Obviously, I'm speaking not of log homes
and outhouses but rather of the substance, the essence, of
the family. *Little House on the Prairie* portrays for us the way
the Christian family lived and functioned throughout all history prior to the sexual revolution that blossomed from the
postwar 1950s era. A family working together to build their
life. Kids knowing where they belong, leaning on their mom
and dad, learning from the younger and the older amongst
them. This theme of mentorship, allowing someone else's
hindsight to become your foresight, is enforced throughout
all of Scripture. These moral, biblical themes are one of the
reasons Charles Ingalls and Laura Ingalls Wilder became
household names in the 1970s. As Christianity became more
and more of a subculture, people felt these ideals slipping
away but were unable to identify what was happening. I
think they have grieved for that deep sense of love and be-
longing ever since.

A mandatory part of simplifying our lives is learning to
set healthy boundaries. This is a hard one, but the reality is
that God did not call us to be everything to everyone, and
when we try to be, quality is sacrificed.

We have, however, concretely and inarguably been given

the children in our care, and living up to the standards of modern society means that parents are working, volunteering, getting involved in sporting events and practices, attending church, and keeping up with responsibilities at home. We are often too overwhelmed (and exhausted!) to think straight, much less get everything accomplished in the way we know it needs to be done.

What happens when we rush through washing the dishes or brushing our teeth? We miss spots. We're living in a world that creates and thrives off chaos. If we aren't intentionally pushing against that chaos, we are driven directly into it, and we miss things. Very important things.

So where do we start? We can teach our children, through our own actions, to slow down and give propaganda and consumerism the attitude it deserves. These aspects of modern life are negative forces with which we must reckon. We can be intentional about making time to equip ourselves properly about life and relationships, love and value—and how all of those things come first from God the Father, through the sacrifice of His Son, Jesus Christ.

That relationship for which Christ was sacrificed, and the incredible value we have because of it, flows through us and into all those around us.

My husband speaks very highly of the fact that his father made it mandatory for him and his brothers to be with him in church and Sunday School every week. Consequently, guess whose children are also in church and Sunday School each week? Ours. Setting aside time to pray together and incorporate family devotions into your nightly bedtime routine is another way we can be intentional about equipping ourselves to face a godless world. We have always read and still do read (even to our teenagers) *Little Visits with God,* a classic family devotional. It contains great stories of faith and real-life examples of facing temptation and struggle that give our kids direction and enforce a faithful mind-set as they grow and learn how to deal with challenges in their own lives.

When we understand the value we have, first because we are created in God's image and foremost because we are baptized into Christ, then we can love and value our neighbor in the same way. Then, through that understanding, we will see that our neighbor is also created in God's image and that Jesus died for his or her sin too. Then, our children will grow up in that context as a people with great regard for human life, so much so that they could never find pleasure in taking advantage of another person's body or in devaluing their own.

IT'S A FRAME OF MIND

We hear it said all the time: "It's just sex."

Every time we do, we have to ask: How can something so consequential be given away so casually as though there aren't any heartstrings attached? It can't.

Referring to sex in such a cavalier manner is comparable to a teenager wolfing down three cheeseburgers, fries, and two cherry pies before soccer practice. It's foolishness. That kid is going to be sick. Nothing good is going to come from it. Yet the "it's just sex" foolishness has all but taken over our families.

Families need this reminder: sexual intimacy and integrity are connected to a deeper biblical wisdom of God's love for His children. We are uniquely created to be in relationship, first with our God and second with the world around us. The respect for that order is missing in the world today. Constant distractions pull us away from profound, personal connection and draw us into the skin-deep, "looks good on the surface," "feels good in the moment" casual sex propaganda. Gone are the days of reading the Bible and studying Scripture. The majority of us are biblically illiterate, and the only one benefiting from it is Satan himself. A major point that I make all throughout this book is that we have a God of *order*. He comes first. He's at the top of the pyramid, and He wills that every single thing in this life be brought to Him. Not because He's a dictator, a Joseph Stalin, Benito Mussolini god, but because of His tremendous love for you. He created order for *our* benefit, not His. That is why we need to pick up our Bibles and know what is contained within.

SCRIPTURE CONNECTION

Long ago, at many times and in many ways, God spoke to our fathers by the prophets, but in these last days He has spoken to us by His Son, whom He appointed the heir of all things, through whom also He created the world. He is the radiance of the glory of God and the exact imprint of His nature, and He upholds the universe by the word of His power. (Hebrews 1:1–3)

If you've ever caught yourself thinking or saying the following things about sex, then you're just like the rest of us sinners and have tried to make your ways God's ways. The joke is on us, as we've all experienced at one time or another, because His ways are never ours, and our ways don't pan out for very long. We need to come before the holy altar where we receive Christ's body, which cleanses our bodies, and His blood, which shoots through our veins, every part of our bodies and souls, and purges the darkness and pride to which we've subscribed so boldly. You've been duped by sexual propaganda if you've accepted any of the following statements as truth:

- "I believe in waiting until I'm married to have sex, but if the right person comes along and we love each other, then it would be okay."

- "As long as my kids are using protection and being responsible, their sex life is none of my business."

- "I was a kid once too. I did it all, and I turned out all right."

- "It's okay to experiment with your sexuality so you can find your true self."

- "What's the big deal? Having sex is part of growing up."

- "Let them get it out of their systems now so when they get married, they won't have any regrets."

- "It makes sense for us, financially, to live together."

- "It's important to live together or sleep together before you get married, so you know that you're compatible with each other."

We've been had, my friends, and it's time to rectify our mind-set. Every one of the above examples is connected. This is a frame of mind that is being ingrained in us, every hour of every day. Like brainwashing. The problem is that this perfunctory line of thinking goes against God's intentions for sex, relationships, healthy marriage, and healthy families. What is commonly referred to as "old-fashioned" and "rigid" is actually the wisdom and provision of a loving

Father who gives His children boundaries in order to keep them happy, healthy, safe, strong, and faithful.

SCRIPTURE CONNECTION

Therefore put away all filthiness and rampant wickedness and receive with meekness the implanted word, which is able to save your souls.

But be doers of the word, and not hearers only, deceiving yourselves. For if anyone is a hearer of the word and not a doer, he is like a man who looks intently at his natural face in a mirror. For he looks at himself and goes away and at once forgets what he was like. But the one who looks into the perfect law, the law of liberty, and perseveres, being no hearer who forgets but a doer who acts, he will be blessed in his doing.

If anyone thinks he is religious and does not bridle his tongue but deceives his heart, this person's religion is worthless. Religion that is pure and undefiled before God the Father is this: to visit orphans and widows in their affliction, and to keep oneself unstained from the world. (James 1:21–27)

Picture in your mind that stove again. There's a reason we stop the child from touching it, and that reason never gets old or outdated or irrelevant.

So it is with biblical sexual integrity.

CHAPTER 1

Discussion Questions

» Why do our children get hurt, even though we do our best to protect them?

» What are some examples of both negative and positive propaganda found in our culture today?

» How has the propaganda of our culture shaped our frame of mind in regard to sex?

» How does God's Word counter that propaganda?

CHAPTER 2

There's No Such Thing as Safe Sex (Outside of Marriage)

A husband meets up with an old high school flame and begins a sexual relationship with her. He has stepped outside of the marriage boundary, or covenant, that he made with his wife and with God. He has taken himself out of the safe harbor and voluntarily sailed into dangerous waters.

A girl makes the choice to engage in oral sex with her boyfriend. In so doing, she has made the choice to open Pandora's box of hurt and disappointment, not to mention her exposure to disease and her growing lack of self-worth with each cheap interaction.

A guy thinks that he simply needs to use a condom, and a girl believes that she only needs to be faithful taking her birth control, and they trust that this practice somehow ensures safe sex. They have placed their full assurance in protecting themselves from only one of the challenges they face when choosing to have sex outside of marriage.

Teens, more than ever, are looking for examples of healthy relationships after which they can model their lives. I haven't met a single teenager yet who hasn't expressed the desire for a healthy marriage and family someday. Take a few minutes and spend some time asking your kids about this. In a perfect world, without divorce, what would their future look like? Divorce has hurt us. It has hurt our families, and it has skewed many of our kids' views on marriage.

The idea that a healthy marriage is unattainable is the foundation of our casual-sex culture. The thought process goes something like this: "My grandparents didn't have a healthy marriage; my parents didn't have a healthy marriage either. Marriage is overrated. Marriage carries no value—it's just a piece of paper. As long as I love the person I'm with, then having sex outside of marriage with him or her is okay."

Basic companionship is almost always at the core of relationships that are based on sex rather than on marriage. The vast majority of teens and college-age kids who are having sex are in monogamous relationships and aren't seeking to be rebellious by any means. They just want someone by their side.

Now, let's briefly clarify all that for a minute: contrary to what fanatics on either end of the spectrum would have us believe, and what the media is more than happy to enable, teenage and young adult culture has not become one giant orgy. By and large, these kids think they have good values and morals, and they foster and care deeply about that.

Millennials may have popularized the hookup culture and the notion of "friends with benefits," but social scientists have made a surprising discovery about the sex lives of these young adults: they're less promiscuous than their parents' generation. According to a recent study in the *Archives of Sexual Behavior*, the average number of sexual partners for Americans born between the 1980s and the 1990s is about the same as for the baby boomers born between 1946 and 1964: 11.68 partners. The millennial generation comes in with a much smaller average of 8.26 sexual partners.[2]

The problem is that they haven't been taught to see the crippling imprint they're leaving on their bodies when one relationship ends and a new one begins. The division and strife becomes a part of them. They have a good cry over a breakup and move on in search of the next true love—because that's what they've been taught to do.

However, they are weaker now, and less trusting of others. Now cynicism grows, and everything they've seen and been told about relationships must be true: that real, unconditional love doesn't exist. That members of the opposite sex can't be trusted. In my experience, this is one of the factors contributing to the increasing appeal of homosexuality as well. Guys and girls feel let down or hurt by their relationships with the opposite sex and are drawn to sex with members of their own gender, because they think they will treat them better.

When we build our relationships on sex first, we are building our futures on the sand instead of on the Rock. We are trying to build a house from a crayon drawing instead of a blueprint. Vital information is missing, and the lack of it will get you only so far.

THE TROUBLE WITH CONDOMS AND BIRTH CONTROL

We are not just a physical body that has physical needs, as modern culture would have us think. We are a whole body made up of emotional, mental, spiritual, and social elements as well.

---

2   Jean M. Twenge, Ryne E. Sherman, Brooke E. Wells, "Changes in American Adults' Sexual Behavior and Attitudes, 1972–2012," *Archives of Sexual Behavior* 44, no. 8 (November 2015), https://link.springer.com/article/10.1007/s10508-015-0540-2 (accessed April 13, 2018).

When we talk about sex in terms of youth, we almost always focus on the following things: birth control, condoms, body image, and the ever-popular human instinct. These things pertain only to the physical aspects of a whole person—the simple one-fifth of the entire person that God created so intricately and intentionally in His image.

Birth control and condoms provide a false sense of security, plain and simple. Parents, the minute you put your daughters on some sort of hormonal birth control, statistically, you increase their risk of contracting a sexually transmitted infection by ten times. Teens hear the words "safe sex" and assume they have nothing else to worry about. How many of the teens in your life are capable of putting their dirty socks in the laundry consistently every day? Or of taking their vitamins without being reminded? Teenagers are more likely to contract sexually transmitted diseases while using birth control or condoms because the more comfortable they get with having sex, the less consistent they become with using protective measures. This false sense of security actually puts our children in harm's way, instead of keeping them safe.

Did you know that an estimated 150 million women worldwide take birth control pills? Such widespread use of chemical hormones worries me, because many women are not aware of the serious health implications of these drugs. I'm aghast at the number of teen girls who are using birth control pills (prescribed by their doctors) to address symptoms such as cramping, spotting, irregular periods, and acne, instead of addressing the underlying causes of the symptoms instead.

Not surprisingly, a report by the Guttmacher Institute reveals that teens between the ages of fifteen and nineteen are more likely to use birth control pills to treat menstrual discomfort than for birth control (82 percent versus 67 percent).[3]

Many women do not consider the very real (and sometimes very dangerous) side effects of these synthetic hormones, but we owe it to our bodies, and to our future children, to take a minute and intentionally think this through. We need to find out more.

I know that on the surface, modern methods of birth control seem like a godsend. We suddenly have so much control over our reproductive cycles. Who wouldn't want that? But hear me out for a minute as we unpack this box together.

First, let's understand how birth control pills work in a woman's body.

Typically, the body ovulates once a month, ripening a new egg that will make its way through a fallopian tube. Seven to ten days after ovulation, on average, the egg reaches the uterus, where it will implant, if fertilized by a sperm. If the egg is not fertilized, then the lining of the uterus that had built up in preparation for the fertilized egg is unnecessary. Both egg and uterine lining leave the body, cleansing the woman's uterus and preparing for a new cycle.

When we take birth control pills, we impose synthetic hormones on our natural cycle. Many birth control pills contain high levels of estrogen that effectively convince the

3   "Many American Women Use Birth Control Pills for Noncontraceptive Reasons," Guttmacher Institute (November 15, 2011), https://www.guttmacher.org/news-release/2011/many-american-women-use-birth-control-pills-noncontraceptive-reasons (accessed April 17, 2018).

pituitary gland that the woman is pregnant (which explains some of the side effects of the drugs) and that she doesn't need to ovulate. Because the body thinks it is pregnant, the uterine lining thickens. Once the woman starts the placebo pills (inactive pills without hormones), however, her estrogen level drops suddenly and her body menstruates "normally."

This abnormal cycle is what millions of women experience every month, yet few doctors discuss the consequences of taking these prescriptions and imposing an unnatural cycle year after year. Below is an overview of the reported risks and side effects of birth control pills and synthetic hormonal birth control methods. Some physical and emotional changes take place that stay with a woman as long as she remains on this type of contraceptive. Many of these changes occur as the body's response to synthetic estrogen. These changes include the following:

- Breast tenderness
- Weight gain
- Reduced or increased acne
- Mood swings
- Shortness of breath

- Vitamin deficiency
- Irregular bleeding or spotting
- Eczema
- Irritable bowel syndrome
- Decreased libido[4]

The above side effects might be enough to deter some women from taking birth control, but many women are just not aware of them, while others justify the side effects because the pill is so convenient.

However, imagine taking your birth control pill, feeling

---

4   Alisa Vitti, "What You Need to Know about Synthetic Birth Control," WellandGood. com, February 23, 2018, https://www.wellandgood.com/good-advice/health-risks-synthetic-birth-control (accessed June 26, 2018).

depressed as a side effect, and then taking an antidepressant to handle your mood swings and hypersensitivity. Adding an antidepressant could then introduce more side effects and complications. My point is that birth control pills are a prescription drug with very real ramifications on a woman's overall health. Also, taking into consideration that 11.01 percent of youth age 12 to 17 in the US reported suffering at least one major depressive episode in 2017[5]—that's over three million kids—we have some very real red flags billowing right before our eyes.

Even scarier than the so-called "mild" side effects are the serious health risks that accompany synthetic hormonal birth control methods. Ladies, we may not mind the annoyances of tender (or bigger) breasts aforementioned, but these items here are the real deal. Serious health risks include the following:

- Increased risk of cervical and breast cancers
- Increased risk of heart attack and stroke
- Migraines
- Higher blood pressure
- Gall bladder disease
- Infertility
- Benign liver tumors
- Decreased bone density
- Yeast overgrowth and infection
- Increased risk of blood clotting[6]

Cancer, heart disease, stroke, infertility. Surely these side effects make birth control pills a less-than-desirable option for contraception. And now that heart disease has

5 "2017 State of Mental Health In America—Youth Data," Mental Health America, http://www.mentalhealthamerica.net/issues/2017-state-mental-health-america-youth-data (accessed April 16, 2018).

6 "Women, Heart Disease and Stroke" (pamphlet), American Heart Association, 2017.

become the leading cause of death among women, one has to wonder if there is a connection with the widespread and long-term use of oral contraceptives—which debuted in 1960, just as the first of the baby boomers were entering their teens.

Yeast overgrowth and yeast infections (candida), too, are particularly dangerous to your overall health. Birth control pills actually destroy the beneficial bacteria in your intestines, making you more susceptible to yeast overgrowth, lower immunity, and infection.

The long and short of it is that birth control has become something that we, as a culture, approach casually. On the surface, it seems to be a good option for preventing unplanned pregnancy among teens, but we sacrifice our girls' total health and well-being when we establish this risky foundation as a standard to be respected and followed. Natural family planning is an incredible option, and one that worked for centuries prior to the birth control revolution. There are many different methods and options from which we can choose, and these should be considered in place of synthetic hormonal birth control.

Working in life-affirming ministry, I've seen firsthand the local numbers that add to the average of 85 percent of US abortions being performed on unmarried women.[7] The way to eliminate these abortions is not by handing out more condoms and birth control. The solution is to give people a better understanding of what abortion actually is and does, as well as a better understanding of how unreliable birth

---

7   Jenna Jerman, Rachel Jones, Tsuyoshi Onda, "Characteristics of U.S. Abortion Patients in 2014 and Changes Since 2008," Guttmacher Institute, https://www.guttmacher.org/report/characteristics-us-abortion-patients-2014 (accessed May 18, 2018).

control can be. Rest assured, if abortion was not so readily available, a lot more singles would think twice about getting into bed together.

Some years ago, in the middle of giving the keynote speech at a pregnancy center banquet, a woman, who was both liberal in her politics and a feminist in that she was pro-abortion, pro-contraception, and pro-women's equality rights, stood up and called me out right in the middle of my presentation. Her grievance that couldn't wait was that birth control, at the very least, should never be withheld from those women living in poverty or from those people with disabilities. She was convinced that what she had to say would change the minds of everyone in the room. That much was unmistakable, as she gave an emotionally charged speech of her own. She didn't feel bad that she had stopped the banquet and called me out, in front of several hundred people, to prove her point.

Honestly, I'm not a fan of confrontation, but this was a time when I had to point out something vitally important: according to the movement she followed, those adults with disabilities would all have been aborted and the women living in poverty were doomed to continue doing so due to a feminist mindset that has all but sucked the masculinity out of our world. I struggle with the hypocrisy of the women's rights movement when that group is, first of all, willing to abort babies who have been deemed unworthy of life by someone else's personal standards and, second, pushes an agenda that will keep over one-quarter of our American women—single moms—in poverty due to a power-hungry desire to outmaneuver men, demasculinize them, and replace them in any way they possibly can.[8]

---

8   Dawn Lee, "Single Mother Statistics," Single Mother Guide, https://singlemother
guide.com/single-mother-statistics" (accessed May 18, 2018).

According to 2017 US Census Bureau, out of about 12 million single-parent families with children under age 18, more than 80 percent were headed by single mothers.[9]

This macho female mind-set over the last four decades has at least contributed to, if not solely supported, the degrading of men to the point that they are no longer respected or called to be respected within the family. A woman can do all the same things a man can do; having been a single mom for a year, I can easily see how women fall into this line of thinking. I felt like I had to do it all. But just because a woman can doesn't mean she should. And that goes for men as well. Just because a man is capable of doing everything on his own doesn't mean he should. Truth be told, we know we're failing when we go at it alone and allow sex to take precedence over marriage. It haunts us with every unpaid bill, every rebellious child, every lonely night, and so on.

God has created us to complement one another so as to mirror Christ's relationship with the Church. In marriage, God, the great Teacher, gives us a visual from which we can learn. Anything that deviates from that picture is a mockery of our relationship with Him. We were never intended to raise a family as single parents. We hear of single moms more frequently because men have been taught, culturally, that they can live like they're married as long as it suits them. A couple can sleep together and have kids together; then, when situations arise calling for strength and wisdom and patience, nothing binds the man to the home, so he leaves. This is the fruition of decades of casual sex, pretending, "playing house" together. Due to the overwhelming

---

9   Lee, "Single Mother Statistics."

focus on women's oppression by men, our sons have been taught to "let the women handle it." People who are pro-choice do not truly advocate for women's rights when they are willing to pick and choose which women live or die or thrive according to standards of convenience and of cultural priority, rather than to God's standards. Biblical women's equality is, ironically, being unequally yoked with their husbands. Yes, women are equal to men in the fact that we are all children of God, fearfully and wonderfully made by a Creator, baptized and redeemed by a Savior. No, we are not equal in the fact that we have been given specific and, frankly, amazingly compatible traits that require us to work in relationship with one another.

As I shared with this woman and the entire room of innocent bystanders, relationships require responsibility, more so if you have someone in your life with a handicap or if you're a single parent with limited access to healthcare. Just as technology has been abused and turned into a baby-sitting service, birth control has been abused and turned into a "get into bed free card" that has led us to neglect caring for one another intimately. Not sexually, *intimately*, in a way that involves detailed knowledge. That woman said we need birth control for handicapped adults and women living in poverty? I say we need to do a better job of loving our neighbor, whoever that might be.

There is no such thing as safe sex outside the confines of marriage. To subscribe to this notion is to build your house on a foundation that's four-fifths void of massively impor-tant details, affecting your future in ways for which no one can prepare. I can't stress this enough: God has thought through every aspect of birth control. He created sex in the first place, and He is the ultimate authority on it. He provides the best contraception methods in abstinence for singles and in natural family planning for married couples. *Simplify.*

MORE THAN JUST A PHYSICAL BODY

You are a whole person. You have a physical body that eats, sleeps, runs, and jumps. You have a mind that thinks and processes and controls your physical body through your central nervous system; this is your mental person. Additionally, you are an emotional person who feels happiness, sadness, anger, resentment, love, contentment, and so many other wonderful emotions. You are also a social person—not in the sense that you are outgoing or love people (that's certainly not true of everyone!), but in the sense that God created you to be in relationship with others. Everywhere you are, have been, or will ever be requires that you interact with those around you. Finally, you are a spiritual person. In the same way that God has created you to interact with fellow human beings, He also created you, at the core of your being, to be in relationship with Him. "Once in the blest baptismal waters I put on Christ and made Him mine; Now numbered with God's son and daughters, I share His peace and love divine" (*LSB* 598:1).[10]

This truth—that we are more than just a physical body wandering aimlessly through the world—is, unfortunately, one of the best kept secrets of our time, and it's not by accident either. You are more than a body with instincts and innate desires that must be met. Your mind controls your

---

10   Text of *LSB* 598 is copyright © 1941 Concordia Publishing House. All rights reserved, Used by permission.

body, not the other way around. That's the reason we've all been able to achieve potty-training.

What God has created to be the single most intimate bond between a man and woman—sex—Satan has twisted and distorted into something that is dangerous and destructive. God knew Satan would do this, so He gave us marriage, an invaluable gift that protects not only our bodies but also our hearts, minds, and spirits. Although it's much easier to justify bad behavior by picturing Him this way, God is definitely not an old man in the sky oppressing us with His traditions from ancient days and forcing us to hold out for sex.

Marriage is the shield God has given us to defend ourselves wholly from the attacks of Satan on our everyday lives and bodies.

PHYSICAL CONSEQUENCES OF SEX OUTSIDE OF MARRIAGE

Within the marriage walls, God has created sex to be an amazing experience between a man and a woman. This should not be diminished or understated in any way. Sex is a great thing! You were created to connect with your spouse, through sexual intercourse, like a five-point puzzle: with your physical body, your mind, your emotions, your spirit, and in how you relate to each other socially. That's awesome! It's an incredible creation of God that cannot be replaced by anything else in this world. That gift is worth striving for, diligently and continuously. That bond is worth putting in some time and thought and prayer.

Unfortunately, outside the confines of marriage, sex becomes dangerous and destructive—and powerful. With great power comes great responsibility. Sex is an incredibly influential act, whether used for good or for evil.

I recently started watching a show where there's an alternate world that exists underneath the real world, called the "Upside Down." In this alternate world, everything looks the same but is gray, dark, and covered in a depressing haze. Dwelling in this abyss is a monster that always seeks to devour new blood and preys on the weaknesses of the characters. It is possible for the show's characters to get out of this sinking underworld alive, but that is difficult and doesn't come without them losing a little bit of themselves.

Casual sex reminds me of the Upside Down. The physical body is an amazing thing. Abused by casual sex, however, this part of you is at risk for some pretty big consequences: unplanned pregnancy, sexually transmitted infections and diseases, infertility, and in some cases, even cancer.

UNPLANNED PREGNANCY

When I was nineteen years old, I found myself mixed up in a life of casual sex and, ultimately, facing an unplanned pregnancy. I say "found myself" because I was lost. I woke up each day and went with the flow. Wherever I was and whatever happened to me was haphazard, usually void of any real thought or intention.

After high school, I went to college, and the world was at my fingertips. No parents, no rules, right? Wrong. There are always rules. We can pretend for a little while that they don't exist, but the consequences are inevitable. In my case, casual sex led me down the road of contemplating whether to bring another life into this world. I was a sophomore in college and in no position to be a mother. The trouble is, I was thinking of my child's life as something that was yet to come, not someone who already was. By the time I was staring down at that pregnancy test, she was already my child, and I was already her mom.

Our nation's own Health and Human Services organization defends life beginning at conception! "HHS accomplishes its mission through programs and initiatives that cover a wide spectrum of activities, serving and protecting Americans at every stage of life, beginning at conception."[11]

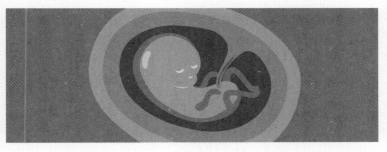

My option moving forward was one of three very difficult decisions:

- I could choose to parent my baby, and my life would change drastically.
- I could make an adoption plan for my baby, and my life would change drastically.
- I could have an abortion, and my life would change drastically.

I will just say, first of all, that no young woman or man should have to face any of these decisions on their own.

11 Nancy Flanders, "HHS to Define Human Life as 'Beginning at Conception,'" Live Action News, https://www.liveaction.org/news/new-hhs-strategic-plan-protects-american-lives-beginning-conception (accessed May 18, 2018). See also "Introduction: About HHS," US Department of Health and Human Services, https://www.hhs.gov/about/strategic-plan/introduction/index.html (accessed May 18, 2018).

This was, hands down, the most stressful and difficult time in my life. If you know someone going through this, give her or him your time and your ear if you can.

If I chose to parent my baby, I would have to tell everyone I was pregnant. That meant exposing my recklessness to the world. And as if that wasn't enough, my mind was swimming with all of the other implications with which I was going to have to deal. What about school? What would my parents and my family think of me? What about money? (I had none.) I could barely take care of myself—I was living the life of spontaneity and fun! Motherhood was definitely not what I had in mind. It was not part of my perfect plan. Well, one thing became clear to me right away. There was no perfection in my plans. I had sinned. I had gotten sidetracked by what I wanted and what felt good for me at the time. Freedom does that if you're not careful.

Scared and very aware of the fact that another human life was now in my hands, I didn't know what I was going to do. If I chose to make an adoption plan, I'd have to find an agency I trusted. Where to begin? As a nineteen-year-old, I hadn't the slightest clue where to go or whom to contact for that. Would I have the nerve and selflessness to look into my child's eyes and give her away to someone else? Could I live my life not knowing where or who she was?

If I chose to have an abortion, there was a clinic close by to my college. There were trained professionals there who could help me so I wouldn't feel alone, and many of my friends had been there before or knew someone who had been. I wouldn't have to tell my family and see the sadness and disappointment on their faces. I could continue on with school, and my life would basically be the same as it was before. Easy peasy.

Except.

She already exists.

I'm already her mom.

I'd be taking away the life of my child.

I chose to parent my daughter, and I had to face up to my poor choices. My whole life up until that crucial decision was all about me. I even tried to make my baby's very own precious life all about me, when the reality is that another person's life is never your own.

Isabella Grace—Bella—was the tiny little person whom God created for so many mighty purposes in this world. It was beyond my power and right to take that from her by stealing her life for my own gain.

My life did change drastically when I found out I was pregnant with Bella. Most of the things I listed above happened. I had to face my family's disappointment and sadness, which over time turned into anticipation and excitement as we welcomed a new member of the family into our lives. I did have to leave the college I was attending and move away from all my friends, but when I moved home, I was surrounded by my big, amazing family instead and was able to take online classes at a local community college. I didn't end up marrying Bella's father, because God showed me something life changing: we all make mistakes. It's what we do after the mistake that determines our character. Repent! And then do the next right thing. God will work out the rest.

He knew how important it was to me to have a healthy marriage and family. One year later, when Matt Ruesch, my childhood friend, and I were sitting across the table from each other on our first date, we both knew we'd be married forever. On August 27, 2001, when Bella was thirteen months old, I married the man she knows as Daddy, and God completed His promise to care for this scared, single mom who chose life. You see, I know many women who have suffered through the pains of abortion. Life doesn't go back to normal. Once you're pregnant, that new life has already affected yours. You will carry that person with you every day—in joy and peace or in resentment and sadness. Just remember: there's no skeleton in the closet that's too old to get rid of. I've sat with women in their sixties and seventies who carried the sin of abortion with them their whole lives and received the forgiveness and healing they needed after going through some wonderful post-abortion counseling at their local Christian pregnancy resource center. These centers are all across America. If you or someone close to you is carrying this burden, or facing an unplanned pregnancy and needs help, there are crisis pregnancy centers all across America that would love to come alongside you to provide honest, accurate information and support. Go to care-net.org and click "Find a Pregnancy Center," or visit optionline.org. An unplanned pregnancy, outside of marriage, is one of the most vulnerable positions in which you can put yourself.

I'd also like to include this final, important detail for when we're talking to the young men in our lives. The way our legal system is set up in the United States, if a young man is unmarried and gets a girl pregnant, he has no say in how she handles that pregnancy. That means dads have no legal rights to their children as long as the baby is in her womb. If she chooses to have an abortion, she can do so without his consent. I have seen so many grieving dads throughout my time as a pro-life advocate. Abortion doesn't affect just the mom and the baby. Dads, grandmas, grandpas, aunts, uncles, friends, teachers, and counselors are affected as well.

SEXUALLY TRANSMITTED INFECTIONS AND DISEASES

Sex was never meant to kill us, guys. If we have sex with only one person, who had sex with two others, who had sex with two others, and so on, then we have been exposed to all of them. Before I go on, if your teen is sexually active, he or she needs to see a doctor to be tested for sexually transmitted infections and diseases (STIs and STDs). (The websites at the end of the previous section can also be resources to help you find confidential clinics in your area for this purpose.[12])

That's his or her reality.

Many people don't realize they are infected, and they pass on diseases without even knowing it. There's a false sense of security that comes with placing condoms and birth control methods in such a lofty position. Condoms cannot protect people from all STDs, and as you will read in the coming pages, every time someone has sex with a person other than his or her spouse, he or she is potentially exposing him- or herself to any number of unknown sexually transmitted infections. Birth control only keeps you from getting pregnant. Trust me when I say that for the person

---

12 Care Net, "Find a Pregnancy Center," https://www.care-net.org/find-a-pregnancy-center (accessed April 16, 2018).

having casual sex outside the safe harbor of marriage, an unplanned pregnancy is probably the least of his or her worries.

There's a profound "sex without attachments" mentality being pushed on our families. A perfect example of this is that we see sex scenes regularly in most television programs and commercials. We hear about it openly in the music we listen to and the movies we go see. But how often can you recall hearing the actor's or singer's woes about the diseases he or she has contracted through the promiscuous lifestyle? The CDC estimates that nearly 20 million new sexually transmitted infections occur every year, accounting for almost 16 billion dollars in health-care costs annually.[13] It's safe to say that there's a whole lot of important but not very glamorous information left out of the media. That is why it's important to know what we're up against. On the following pages, I've written a quick description of the most common sexually transmitted infections for men and women in the United States.

There are two categories of infections contracted through sexual contact—STIs (sexually transmitted infections) that develop into STDs (sexually transmitted diseases). They are symptomatic and asymptomatic. This is really important. *Symptomatic* means the infections present with symptoms, so the individual knows he or she has contracted a disease and can seek treatment, though not necessarily a cure. *Asymptomatic* means that the infection does not present with symptoms, so the individual doesn't know he or she has contracted a disease until it causes further damage in his or her body.

---

13   Centers for Disease Control and Prevention, "Reported STDs in the United States," https://www.cdc.gov/std/stats13/std-trends-508.pdf (accessed April 16, 2018).

I've also included the various ways humans can contract these infections. Remember that these are the most commonly contracted STIs in the United States. There are others that I don't go into here.

Ladies and gentlemen, you cannot pick your sexually transmitted infection or disease. There's a gravely false sense of security when we view condoms as protection. Every time a person thinks he or she is being responsible and practicing safe sex by using a condom or only engaging in oral sex, that person is still putting him- or herself at risk for contracting any number of diseases that can be spread through simple skin-to-skin genital contact, in whatever combination one can think of. Oral sex is not safe sex, just as using condoms and birth control is not safe sex.

HPV (HUMAN PAPILLOMAVIRUS)

HPV is the most common sexually transmitted infection in the United States today. There are more than forty types of viruses that can be spread through vaginal, anal, or oral sex. They can be contracted through simple skin-to-skin contact as well.

Some strains of HPV can cause genital warts, while others infect the mouth and throat. HPV is the leading cause of cervical cancer and cancer of the penis, mouth, or throat.

HPV is, in most cases, asymptomatic.

The HPV Vaccine

There has been a lot of talk about vaccines that can protect youth from contracting the human papillomavirus. I want to take a minute to set the record straight here. These vaccines are called Cervarix, Gardasil, and Gardasil 9, and they can protect against strains that cause genital warts, some types of vaginal cancer, and some types of anal cancer.

The CDC recommends that young women ages 11 to 26 and young men ages 11 to 21 be vaccinated for HPV.[14]

There's much controversy about vaccines in general, so let's start there. If you are a person who tends to vaccinate your children according to CDC guidelines, you will find that the risks associated with the HPV vaccine are similar to those associated with the other vaccinations administered to your child. That is, though it is very rare, vaccines can cause side effects such as allergic reactions, immune system damage, or other complications. I think the dilemma for parents who struggle with whether to vaccinate their children against HPV is this: the HPV vaccination needs to be considered only if your child is going to have sex outside of marriage. Determining that at the age of eleven is a grueling and risky position to be in as a parent and as a child.

Might I suggest we shift the focus, then, to instructing our children, intentionally and passionately, both on the value of marriage and on what it means to have sexual integrity, starting before the age of eleven and for all their years to come? In my experience, a child who recognizes the value of his or her sexuality and of all human life is much less likely to abandon it later as a teen and into adulthood. There is a risk either way, and this risk needs to be considered by parents according to their individual situation and with full knowledge of what is at stake. Have the tough conversation with your kids: "Would you consider dating someone if you knew that he or she had been sexually active already? If so, what risks and responsibilities might come with that?" As a

---

14 Centers for Disease Control and Prevention, "HPV Vaccination Recommendations," https://www.cdc.gov/vaccines/vpd/hpv/hcp/recommendations.html (accessed April 16, 2018).

talking point, let your kids know that if they find themselves engaged to a person who has been sexually active within the previous five years, their partner needs to be tested for STDs and cleared or treated before they are married.

CHLAMYDIA

Chlamydia is the most commonly reported STD in the United States. It is, however, ironically referred to as the "silent STD" because about 75 percent of women experience no symptoms while infected and thus never seek treatment. It is a bacterium that spreads through vaginal, anal, or oral sex. A pregnant woman with chlamydia can give the infection to her baby during childbirth. If diagnosed, it can be treated with antibiotics. But again, most people never know they are infected. Chlamydia may result in infertility and various cancers of the reproductive system.[15] It is, in most cases, asymptomatic.

GONORRHEA

Gonorrhea is another bacterial STD, similar to chlamydia and usually found together. A person can get gonorrhea by having vaginal, anal, or oral sex with a partner who has gonorrhea. A pregnant woman with gonorrhea can give the infection to her baby during childbirth. [16]

Most men will experience symptoms, while most women do not. As is common with bacterial infections, symptoms

---

15   Centers for Disease Control and Prevention, "2016 Sexually Transmitted Diseases Surveillance: Chlamydia," https://www.cdc.gov/std/stats16/chlamydia.htm (accessed May 15, 2018).

16   Centers for Disease Control and Prevention, "2016 Sexually Transmitted Diseases Surveillance: Gonorrhea," https://www.cdc.gov/std/stats16/Gonorrhea.htm (accessed May 15, 2018).

include an unusual discharge from the penis or vagina or a burning sensation while urinating. If diagnosed, gonorrhea can be treated with antibiotics; however, it is rarely treated in women, leading to short-term and long-term consequences. Gonorrhea is a common cause of Pelvic Inflammatory Disease (PID) in women. Women with PID won't necessarily have symptoms. PID can damage the fallopian tubes enough to cause infertility, increase risk of ectopic pregnancy, and lead to chronic pain in the pelvic floor or abdomen. Aside from the negative reproductive effects, gonorrhea can spread to the blood or joints and can be life threatening. In men, gonorrhea can cause a painful condition in the tubes attached to the testicles. In rare cases, this can lead to the man becoming sterile (infertile). People with gonorrhea can more easily contract HIV, the virus that causes AIDS, and those infected with HIV and gonorrhea at the same time are far more likely to transmit HIV to someone else.[17]

In most cases, gonorrhea is symptomatic in men and asymptomatic in women.

SYPHILIS[18]

Syphilis is also a bacterium that is often referred to as the "great imitator." In its primary stage, the main symptom is a sore that could be confused for an ingrown hair, a harmless lump, or a cut. Syphilis is contracted by having vaginal, anal, or oral sex with someone who has syphilis. An infected

---

17 Centers for Disease Control and Prevention, "Gonorrhea—CDC Fact Sheet," https://www.cdc.gov/std/gonorrhea/stdfact-gonorrhea.htm (accessed April 16, 2018).

18 Centers for Disease Control and Prevention, "2016 Sexually Transmitted Diseases Surveillance: Syphilis," https://www.cdc.gov/std/stats16/Syphilis.htm (accessed May 15, 2018).

mother is most likely to transmit the infection to her un-born baby via the bloodstream.

The secondary stage of the infection presents with a body rash, followed by sores in the mouth, vagina, or anus. Having four stages in total, all symptoms usually disappear by the third, or latent, stage. The bacteria may lie dormant for years or for the rest of the infected person's life.

Although rare, it can cause organ, nerve, and brain damage. If diagnosed, syphilis can be treated with antibiotics in most cases. Syphilis is, in most cases, asymptomatic.

HERPES[19]

Genital herpes is common in the United States. More than one out of every six people age 14 to 49 years has genital herpes. There are two strains of the herpes virus: HSV-1 and HSV-2. Both can cause genital herpes, but most often the HSV-2 strain causes this infection. Herpes is easy to catch. It is contracted by having vaginal, anal, or oral sex with someone who is already infected. Herpes can also be contracted through skin-to-skin contact. A person is most contagious when he or she has blisters (in or around their mouth, vagina, or anus), but the presence of blisters is not necessary to pass the virus on to someone else. Herpes is a virus, so there is no cure, but medications are available for managing symptoms. Herpes is, in most cases, asymptomatic.

TRICHOMONIASIS[20]

Trichomoniasis is a parasite and one of the most com-

---

19 Centers for Disease Control and Prevention, "2016 Sexually Transmitted Diseases Surveillance: Other Sexually Transmitted Diseases," https://www.cdc.gov/std/stats16/other.htm (accessed April 16, 2018).

20 Centers for Disease Control and Prevention, "Trichomoniasis—CDC Fact Sheet,"

mon treatable STDs in the United States. It is contracted by having vaginal sex with someone who is already infected. It is not common for the parasite to infect other parts of the body such as the hands, mouth, or anus. Women can give it to each other when their genital areas touch.

Trichomoniasis is treatable with antibiotics, but most people do not present with any symptoms. Trichomoniasis is, in most cases, asymptomatic.

HIV/AIDS[21]

HIV, the human immunodeficiency virus, is the virus that causes AIDS. It's passed through body fluids such as blood, semen, vaginal fluids, and breast milk. It can be contracted through vaginal or anal sex with a person who is already infected, by sharing a needle with someone who is infected, or through nursing. HIV cannot be passed through saliva or by kissing. HIV is, in most cases, asymptomatic.

The symptoms of HIV can differ from person to person, and some people may not get any symptoms at all for many years. In the early stages of HIV infection, it's common to have no symptoms. One in five people in the United States with HIV don't know that they even have it, which is why it's so important to get tested, especially if a person has had unprotected sex with more than one partner or has used intravenous drugs. Condoms do prevent the spread of HIV; however, as I said earlier, there's no way to tell with which sexually transmitted infections you will come into contact.

---

https://www.cdc.gov/std/trichomonas/stdfact-trichomoniasis.htm (accessed April 16, 2018).

21   Centers for Disease Control and Prevention, "STDs and HIV—CDC Fact Sheet," https://www.cdc.gov/std/hiv/stdfact-std-hiv.htm (accessed April 16, 2018).

Condoms will not protect you from them all. Commonly, a mild fever is accompanied by flu-like symptoms such as fatigue, swollen lymph glands, and a sore throat. Fatigue can be both an early and later sign of HIV.

These are just a sampling of the most common sexually transmitted infections currently diagnosed in the United States. There's some serious stuff that, if left untreated, can result in infertility, cancer, and even death. Again, you can't pick your STD. Being infected is not like a buffet where you can walk up, select what you want, and reject what you don't. Anyone who is sexually active can get an STD. A person doesn't even have to have oral, anal, or vaginal sex to contract an infection. For example, herpes and HPV are spread by skin-to-skin contact; actual penetration isn't required.

STDs are common, especially among young people. As we said earlier, there are about 20 million new cases each year in the United States. Half of those infections occur in people between age 15 and 24.[22] The CDC estimates that undiagnosed STIs cause twenty-four thousand women to become infertile each year, with untreated chlamydia and gonorrhea infections being the cause of pelvic inflammatory disease (PID) and infertility. If the disease goes untreated, about 10 to 15 percent of women with chlamydia will develop PID. Chlamydia can also cause fallopian tube infection without any symptoms. PID and "silent" infection in the upper genital tract may cause permanent damage to the

---

22 Centers for Disease Control and Prevention, "CDC Fact Sheet: Information for Teens and Young Adults: Staying Healthy and Preventing STDs," https://www.cdc.gov/std/life-stages-populations/stdfact-teens.htm (accessed April 16, 2018).

fallopian tubes, uterus, and surrounding tissues, which can lead to infertility.[23]

With infertility and cancer rates on the rise, it's evident that the facts prove the logic. Certain high-risk types of human papillomavirus (HPV) can cause cervical cancer in women. In men, HPV infection can lead to the development of penile cancers. HPV also can cause cancers of the mouth, throat, and anus in both sexes.[24]

Waiting for marriage and remaining monogamous in marriage are the safest, healthiest ways to enjoy all the good things that sex has to offer.

THE REST OF ME: MENTAL, EMOTIONAL, SOCIAL, AND SPIRITUAL

Wow. That's a lot of information about the physical consequences of casual sex! It's a lot to take in, I know. Yet the information about STIs and unplanned pregnancy is important for parents, youth leaders, and especially teens. They should be discussed and spoken of in conjunction with the rest of the body. But actually, these implications shouldn't be our main focus. A teenage guy or girl who is having sex with a girlfriend or boyfriend is not operating solely on the physical level; their sexual actions affect their whole being. What's going on in their minds and hearts and spirits? Sex plays into those parts of the body with the same amount of impact and importance.

Everywhere I speak with youth, I ask them this question:

---

23 Centers for Disease Control and Prevention, "STDs and Infertility," https://www.cdc.gov/std/infertility/default.htm (accessed April 16, 2018).

24 "HPV and Cancer," National Cancer Institute, https://www.cancer.gov/about-cancer/causes-prevention/risk/infectious-agents/hpv-fact-sheet (accessed May 18, 2018).

"When your friend is having sex with their boyfriend or girl-friend, what does that create?" Here's a hint: no one has *ever* said the words "true love" to me. Actually, the responses are along these lines:

Mental/Thoughts—Worry, fear, stress, regret, low self-esteem, confusion

Emotional/Feelings—Emptiness, loneliness, broken heart, anger, rage, sadness, depression, guilt, shame

Social/Relationships—Reputation, conflict with my parents, avoiding my parents, withdrawal, change in friends, loss of friends

Spiritual/Relationship with God—Guilt, regret, shame, sorrow, alienation, separation, withdrawal

Is it any wonder our youth are struggling with depression, self-harm, and overwhelming stress? Our culture is pushing them to believe that sex is something as casual and meaningless as what outfit they put on that day, and yet the ramifications they carry with them after the fact are anything but casual.

And thus, the cycle begins.

CHAPTER 2

Discussion Questions

» Why is the marriage boundary important?

» What sort of questions confront a girl facing an unplanned pregnancy? How can you help her answer her questions?

» To what is the culture referring when they talk about using protection and having safe sex? There is no such thing as safe sex outside of marriage. Why?

» Do you believe that the Bible is the timeless Word of God? Where does Scripture back this up?

» What are the deceptions of viewing sex as something that is casual and laid-back?

CHAPTER 3

Pornography, Modesty, and Sexual Propaganda

THE MENTALITY OF THE BODY

There are some unbelievable things to be said about the pornography and the fashion industries that can't be over-looked when speaking from the context of sexual propaganda and media influences. The facade, or salesmanship, we put on as a culture in order to make a profit has gotten so out of hand that our kids literally cannot tell the differ-ence between what's real and what's enhanced, modified, or staged.

Not only are the expectations these industries have placed on these men and women, on us all, completely unat-tainable, but they also distract from the divine design and purpose that God intends for the human body. It's gotten to the point that we're ashamed of every organic intention and purpose of the body because it doesn't meet society's standard of *sexuality*.

Sex was never meant to be the main focus. The physical attraction to breasts, muscles, and curves was never meant to surpass God's first priority in creating them. All of those physicalities lend themselves to the making of a healthy marriage, which produces children and sustains a family, and that then emphasizes for us the greatest relationship we will ever experience: the one between us and our Creator, our heavenly Father.

Look with me at Proverbs 31. As you read, notice the assistance that our physical body lends to our entire person. Additionally, this text is a great model for Christian women to look to, and it speaks powerfully of Christian marriage and the way that men should properly view and respect women without objectifying them by their sexuality.

> An excellent wife who can find?
>   She is far more precious than jewels.
> The heart of her husband trusts in her,
>   and he will have no lack of gain.
> She does him good, and not harm,
>   all the days of her life.
> She seeks wool and flax,
>   and works with willing hands.
> She is like the ships of the merchant;
>   she brings her food from afar.
> She rises while it is yet night
>   and provides food for her household
>   and portions for her maidens.
> She considers a field and buys it;
>   with the fruit of her hands she plants a vineyard.
> She dresses herself with strength
>   and makes her arms strong.
> She perceives that her merchandise is profitable.
>   Her lamp does not go out at night.
> She puts her hands to the distaff,
>   and her hands hold the spindle.
> She opens her hand to the poor

and reaches out her hands to the needy.
She is not afraid of snow for her household,
   for all her household are clothed in scarlet.
She makes bed coverings for herself;
   her clothing is fine linen and purple.
Her husband is known in the gates
   when he sits among the elders of the land.
She makes linen garments and sells them;
   she delivers sashes to the merchant.
Strength and dignity are her clothing,
   and she laughs at the time to come.
She opens her mouth with wisdom,
   and the teaching of kindness is on her tongue.
She looks well to the ways of her household
   and does not eat the bread of idleness.
Her children rise up and call her blessed;
   her husband also, and he praises her:
"Many women have done excellently,
   but you surpass them all."
Charm is deceitful, and beauty is vain,
   but a woman who fears the Lord is to be praised.
Give her of the fruit of her hands,
   and let her works praise her in the gates. (Proverbs
31:10–31)

Did you notice how the entire person—physical body, mental, emotional, social, and spiritual—is portrayed in this passage? When we focus our attention only on sex and the superficial features of the body, we neglect all the other attributes of a person that cause us to respect her or him and her or his life in relationship to our own.

The stereotypical woman of faith usually ends up being

portrayed as a weak doormat, a slave to the man she married. But according to Proverbs 31, this woman is no pushover! This woman is strong. She is savvy, respected by men and women alike. Loved by her children, confident in her capabilities, she works hard to provide for them. She is both independent and dependent on her husband. And best of all, she is thankful at the end of the day for the praise and love she receives from her family.

Here is the partnership that is shamed in our culture. Men, this is the woman you sell out in exchange for that lustful brush with the pornography industry. Truly, every time we allow sex to be our mini god, we hold Satan's hand in robbing women of their true identity in Christ. Women, the same thing goes for us: every time we allow vanity to be our mini god, we affirm the lie that Satan so desperately wants us to believe—that we are worth nothing without our looks.

Satan has always intended to separate us from God, just like he did with Jesus in the wilderness.

TEACH YOUR TEENAGERS THIS:

> Satan's mind games and manipulations are the greatest form of spiritual warfare there is. If he can isolate you from your Lord, get you feeling like you're all alone in the world, then you are weakened. The truth is that God never leaves you. He sends His number-one player, our big Brother, so to speak—Jesus Christ—to find you in the midst of the crowd and carry you back to the Father's side every time.

Satan just kept badgering Jesus relentlessly, "If You are truly the Son of God, command those stones to turn into bread." "If You are truly the Son of God, throw Yourself off this temple and see if God saves You." "If You just bow down and worship me, I will give You anything You could ever want: kingdoms and all their glory" (Matthew 4:1–11, paraphrased).

Man, this guy is DESPERATE! He will go to any length to tear us away from the goodness of God—like a little kid who wants all the best players to be on his team. He is fiercely competitive with God and relentless in his pursuit for our loyalty. How better to get it than to fixate on our weaknesses? Whether by temptation, manipulation, bribery, or blackmail, he knows that if he can divert our attention to the superficial pleasures in life, we will consume ourselves with chasing our tails all day long and never have time to stop, reorient, and think deeper.

In advocacy sessions, during my years working in crisis pregnancy centers, I'd ask clients to complete the following exercise in order to prove this theory. Humor me and try it out:

> Right now, you're feeling empty, stressed, depressed, distant, or confused by something in your life. Take a moment and write it down on a piece of paper. Now begin unpacking it. Dig deeper into it. What is the core of the problem? Where is the source of the negative emotion coming from? Are there solutions that stand out to you right away? Is there someone who might be able to help you find a solution? When did it begin? Does it escalate? Is it triggered at times? Are you in need of repentance and forgiveness?

Upon completion of that exercise, after taking the time to think more deeply, do you feel some resolve and peace just knowing that you're on the road to rectifying this inner conflict? Not only do we bridge the spiritual gap with God when we slow down and process our thoughts, but we're also teaching our minds to think in a more mature and well-rounded manner.

All of this matters because it is essential that we, as Christians, are able to discern the mini gods and the antics of Satan from the one true God and His intended identity for both men and women. Every time we make sex or vanity our god, we are playing the game on Satan's team, and pretty soon he's giving us a shirt with our name on it. Before we know it, we're having so much fun that we've lost sight of our Father's team. Now we're panicking. Fear is setting in. Where is He? Where did He go? Did He just leave me here? What kind of Father just leaves His child? He must not care about me at all. I'm worthless. Replaceable.

Enter the sex industry. Prostitution, sex trafficking, porn, and yes, I'm throwing the fashion and marketing industries in there as well. The human desires to be found and loved are real and incredibly powerful. The topics of sex addiction, porn, and self-pleasure are directly linked with that of modesty and vanity. They all displace our focus onto sex and the superficialities of the physical body rather than the whole body in its entirety as God created. Both pornography and vanity pull sex out of God's beautiful intended place and purpose, and they bust it open like a piñata. A moment of feeling good about yourself followed by the stomachache and the realization that it's all gone. It's empty. *You're empty.*

SELF-ESTEEM: KNOWING YOUR VALUE

I've always struggled with my self-esteem. I look at my teenage daughter now and am so incredibly proud of the beautiful woman she's become. I so wish that I could have seen myself that way when I was her age. The things that make her beautiful to me have very little to do with her physical appearance. She is confident and determined. She works hard to get the things she wants in life and doesn't expect handouts. She is generous with her time and loyal to God, her family, and her friends. All of that makes her one of the most stunningly beautiful women in the world.

We know in our spirits that true beauty is rarely ever about physical appearance, but somewhere between our heart and our head we get derailed and begin comparing ourselves with everyone else around us. Especially women, but men as well.

There's a fabulous illustration I heard once about a little puppet who lived in a village where all the people would spend their days placing either stars or dots on one another. If you received stars, that meant people liked you and you were accepted. If you received dots, well, you weren't as significant. This little puppet received dots every day from the other villagers, and because of that, he was very self-conscious and sad. Then he paid a visit to the puppet maker who had made them all, and the puppet maker told the puppet how uniquely and intentionally he was created. Then the puppet realized his life wasn't about what other people thought of him or what he looked like at all! The puppet maker hadn't made any mistakes—he had crafted the puppet exactly the way he wanted him to be and loved him every bit as much as he loved all of his other creations.

This was my children's favorite story when they were younger. When the little puppet finally understood his value to his creator, all the dots fell right off him. My kids' eyes would light up, and I knew that they got it. When God says that we should be like little children in Matthew 18:3, this is one of the things He's talking about! Little children don't doubt the love of their father—but exposure to the sin-darkened world causes teenagers and adults to doubt. We learn to doubt ourselves, others, and even God. Lord, have mercy. Hear me now: The world does not need another one of anybody else. The world needs you and me and all the people everywhere. We're each a piece of the puzzle that God is constructing, and it will never be complete without you.

MODESTY

All right. Modesty. Sigh.

The conflict between every teenage girl and her mother, the focus of many a youth group Bible study, and the bane of every principal's existence.

First of all, let's identify what the word *modesty* implies. According to Merriam-Webster dictionary, modesty is the behavior, manner, or appearance intended to avoid impropriety or indecency—with synonyms such as unpretentiousness, simplicity, and plainness.[25]

It's a good word! It carries value and importance in so many ways. Unfortunately, what I just interpreted is that modesty is plain and boring. It's one of those words that's been overused to the point that our teenagers tune us out when they hear it. At least, that's my impression. Our youth want to be faithful, but they also want to be real. We'd be lying if we, as adults, said we didn't like listening to Christian music *and* Nirvana too sometimes. (Insert your own favorite rock band.) We use swear words more often than we're

---

25 Adapted from "Modesty," Merriam-Webster.com, https://www.merriam-webster.com/dictionary/modesty (accessed April 17, 2018).

comfortable with, and there are some Sunday mornings when the thought of going to church makes us want to cry. Out of dread, not joy.

Christians are human! It is okay to be real, and it's actually really important for us to model that for our kids. They need to see us struggle with sin, repentance, and forgiveness. They need to see us strike the balance between being in this world but not of it. That is a work in progress, by the way; we're all in it together!

I prefer to call it like it is. I am a sinner—a little sassy sometimes, a little indulgent, a little selfish, a little competitive. The list goes on. Why do we expect our children to be a more perfect version of ourselves? That is what we do, isn't it? As parents and even as adults working with youth, we tend to place expectations on the kids in our lives out of regret from our pasts and inflated criteria for behavior. We want our daughters to be prom queens and our sons to be quarterbacks.

The reality is that not one of us was made in the exact image of our earthly parents. And that's okay! God ensures that our families are filled with people of all personalities, interests, and abilities. What a comfort to know that as my family legacy continues, my children will contribute in a way that no one has ever done before, just as I have and my mother before me. That is the real deal. That is true authenticity.

In the same way, our children have weaknesses just like we do. For example, every day before I leave the house, my goal is to look presentable. That's it. This is a standard I've intentionally implemented for myself, knowing that I can get hung up on vanity. I will not allow myself to think any further about it, because the temptation for me to hyperfocus on my looks is intense.

When I was a teenager, it was this focus on appearances that caused me to be extremely critical of my weight, my looks, and ultimately my total value. I struggled with diets, bulimia, and promiscuity, and the whole time I considered myself to be a good Christian, attending church and participating in youth groups and youth rallies.

It is completely normal for me to hear this same story from teenage girls when I am out speaking to groups. Completely normal. Many of our youth today are carrying on a trend I can relate to from my own teen years: the art of intentionally keeping their church friends separate from their school friends. (This is where I plug the great benefits of a Christian school system!) My faith was something that I always kept in its own sphere. My school friends knew that I prayed and went to church, but they knew nothing of my daily, often momentary, dependence on God. Likewise, my church friends knew that I loved music and hated math, but I kept them in the dark, completely, about my struggles to fit in and feel comfortable in my own skin and how that manifested in my relationships with others.

This clashing of the worlds often ends up in a twisted version of Christianity. It's a version that says, "I believe in God, but . . ." or "as long as I'm a good person . . ." It's this lazy religion that caused me to have sex with my boyfriend and then ask God to forgive me. It's this casual faith that led me to believe that showing more skin, having a better body, or wearing the right clothes somehow would make me more beautiful so people would look up to me.

My husband and I were at a Christian music festival a few summers ago when we coined the phrase "Boobs for

Jesus." I know that's a little brash, but this was madness. Listen, a tank top is a tank top, but the way these (Christian logo) tanks were being worn, they certainly had very little to do with advertising the Gospel. It was embarrassing, not just for all of these young ladies but also for the parents who allowed them to leave the house that way as well as for all of us festivalgoers who were completely distracted by, yes, the lack of modesty. And more than that, we were saddened by their vanity. The vainglory that prompted them to want to be looked at, admired, and lusted over for their physical attributes rather than their absolutely stunning value in Christ is directly linked with the lies of Satan, who wishes to distract us from anything of purpose in this world.

I really don't believe that a lack of modesty is the main issue at hand. I'm willing to bet that the majority of people who knew me back then (minus a few in my inner circle) would have said I was a modest young woman. I got good grades, was respectful to others, and was involved in extracurricular activities.

Vanity was the issue back then, and it's still the issue now. Sexual propaganda has taught us to focus on the superficial rather than the resonance of a person—wholly deep, full, and reverberating. It's not about the clothes. It's about the intentions of the person wearing the clothes. I have seen young ladies wearing bikinis on the beach or at the pool who simply like wearing bikinis and are exuding absolutely no sexual energy at all. On the other hand, I have seen women of all ages wearing a turtleneck, jeans, and boots who are flauntingly seeking attention. Yes, my daughters are allowed to wear two-piece bathing suits and leggings. They cannot wear itsy-bitsy-teeny-weeny string bikinis, and they'd better

have on a shirt that covers their backsides if they're wearing leggings—an agreement that works for and respects the
identity of our family. We've implemented commonsense
boundaries, for all of us, that everyone can live with.

My family knows that I have struggled with vanity and
body image my whole life. Rather than pretend that I don't,
we talk about it and learn from one another and hold one
another accountable. I have learned so much about caring
for my mind and body simply by trying to guard my daughters' hearts from the vanity of this world. I do, however, feel
like there's a place for fashion and modesty to meet in the
middle and result in an ability to be comfortable with who
you are without being a distraction to people around you.
Having said that, if either of my daughters were at a place in
her life where we felt she was seeking after increasing sexual
attention or affirmation, we would tighten the rules and
focus on coming alongside her in this area. My first question wouldn't be, "Why is she wearing that?" It would be,
"What's going on that's causing a change in my daughter's
behavior?"

There's a lot of emphasis placed on the clothes women
wear (or don't wear), the way we do our makeup or hair,
and how much or how little we weigh. I am inspired when
I see women of all ages embracing their identity in Christ
before anything else in this world, because when that is in
order, the materialistic and superficial things fall into their
respective places. I always say, "When we put yuck in, yuck
comes out. When we fill our minds with good things, the
things of God, then good things come out." We have to train
ourselves, both in a long-term way and on a day-by-day
basis, to focus on our character and relationship in Christ

instead of our looks. Make good and healthy choices—in all things! With food, clothing, relationships, lifestyle, finances, work, and so on. You get the picture. Take time to pray and study the Bible—it's the fuel in our tank. We can't run on empty. Our lives are about so much more than the vanity and superficialities this world is handing out. Remember, little eyes are watching you and taking it all in. Teach them well, even as you continue to learn yourself.

PORNOGRAPHY AND SELF-PLEASURE

Porn addiction is the fastest-growing addiction in our country, and one of the most hidden. "This thing doesn't go away; it's like cancer in the brain, but it's cancer in the thoughts instead." Truer words were never spoken. (These words are from a recovering pornography addict).

Sexually speaking, we've all heard that men are more visually stimulated and women are more emotionally stimulated. While this physiological difference between men and women is important to remember as we delve into the world of pornography and self-gratification, it can't be used as a justification for acts that are detrimental to our relationship with God, ourselves, and others we care about. Because of the graphic and visual nature of pornography, studies show that abuse or addiction is a strong risk, similar to that of drug or alcohol addiction. Pornography can have a major impact on a person's personal life and work, leading to significant distress and feelings of shame. Excessive use of pornography is one of the main features identified in many people with compulsive sexual behavior.[26]

26 Valerie Voon, Thomas Mole, Paula Bianca, et al., "Neural Correlates of Sexual Cue Reactivity in Individuals with and without Compulsive Sexual Behaviours," *PLOS*

I am commonly referred to as an "anti-porn Christian," and my beliefs on this topic fall within the stereotype that self-pleasure and porn put youth at risk for future addictions. This is something our society seems to think is joke-worthy. Yet I believe that the facts and common sense speak for themselves. Here's where I'm coming from: cliché or not, dabbling in such things stimulates a gratification place in the brain and body, which in fact opens the physiological door to addiction. For example, we know that heroin is a highly addictive drug that releases the same neurochemicals into our bodies that are activated when watching porn, masturbating, or having a sexual experience.[27]

Unfortunately, over my years of teaching abstinence education, I've heard it said many times that masturbation and pornography are harmless ways that men can actually support an abstinent lifestyle decision. I have had many discussions with parents who felt that their teenage son was better off indulging in self-pleasure than having sex with his girlfriend. He's not, by the way. Your son is not better off. He's actually more likely to have sex, and he's going to be having it sooner rather than later because he will have activated a cycle of abuse. Upon engaging in one sexual activity, it isn't long before we tire of it and seek the next big rush. This is science.

Picture for a moment the first time you held hands with your boyfriend or girlfriend. What happened? Butterflies in your stomach, you began to sweat a little bit, quite possibly your mouth went dry or you had a flush of heat to your face.

ONE 9, no. 7 (July 11, 2014), https://doi.org/10.1371/journal.pone.0102419 (accessed April 18, 2018).

27 David J. Ley, "No, Dopamine Is Not Addictive," Psychology Today, https://www.psychologytoday.com/blog/women-who-stray/201701/no-dopamine-is-not-addictive (accessed April 18, 2018).

These are symptoms that chemicals and hormones have just been released into your body. God gave us these chemicals and hormones to help us bond with another human being. But pretty soon, holding hands no longer generates such a rush, does it? However, kissing does. After that, first base, and so on until we are dependent on and distracted by the physical feeling these acts invoke rather than the meaning behind why God created our bodies to function the way they do.

In short, if your son is watching porn, it won't be long before he wants to experience it in real life for himself. Again, that's science as much as it is sin and temptation. Any kind of sex, outside the confines of marriage, is abusive to the sacred nature of our created bodies.

I have even had the benefits of self-pleasure justified for me, in conjunction with a vow of celibacy, by a Catholic priest who, upon hearing me out, found himself in need of Christ's mercy and a new approach to his celibate lifestyle.

I've said it before and I'll say it again: We are sinful, fallen people in need of a Savior. Our human nature causes us to justify our bad behavior in any way we can make sense of it.

When it comes to the sex industry, two things stand out to me as top priority:

- When we stack the value of every single human life against all the other things this world has to offer, the temptation to sin still remains. However, it becomes much easier to rectify the temptation than to follow through with the sin. Get some help. I'm not saying that a Christian miraculously no longer feels aroused by porn after understanding God's value of human life. I'm saying that once things are in perspective, accountability is more easily accepted and attained.

- Parents, the science behind both sex addiction and drug addiction is exactly the same. If you're okay with independent sexual acts (viewing pornography, masturbation), you are literally saying that you're okay with substance abuse as well. We might as well tell our children to go snort a line of heroin. Like drug addicts, sex addicts become addicted to the feelings they get when certain chemical changes occur in the brain. Very often, they will actually turn to substance abuse to either heighten or cope with their emotions of shame and remorse after engaging in sexual behavior. It's a vicious cycle.

Obviously, the best way to handle a pornography addiction or a child who doesn't see the risk involved in masturbation is to focus your teaching and instruction of the child on the value of *people*—first, their own value as sinners for whom Jesus sacrificed Himself, and second, the value of women and men as individuals, not objects.

> When trying to impart the gravity of Christ's death in conjunction with their lives as teens, it's very helpful to pull it apart for them. "Picture it. Jesus Christ is being crucified in this day and age, here, today. He is dragged through town, naked, beaten, and bloody, and as along a parade route, the people are lined up to mock Him. They are yelling and throwing things at Him. The only thing He did wrong was take the blame for your sins upon Himself. His gentle eyes lock with yours as He makes His way through the streets. You watch as they pound nails in His hands and feet; the full weight of His body hangs from them as the cross is lifted from the ground, and He dies. That is the King you serve. If He did all of that for you, don't you think He's going to do everything He can to protect you from evil while you're still here on this earth?"

Additionally, this is an addiction, and it needs to be treated as such. Just as we wouldn't overlook or downplay a drug addiction, we have to be as diligent and responsible with a sex or pornography addiction. There are great resources for Christian counseling all across America. Focus on the Family's counseling department (www.focusonthe family.com) has resources and a listing of Christian therapists in your area to come alongside you as you seek a treatment option that works best for your family or situation.

The hardest aspect of this battle is the secrecy of it. It requires an extreme amount of diligence on the part of the parent, pastor, or youth leader to identify warning signs and then to be able to open up an effective conversation about it with a teen. The best approach is always the proactive one. Teaching, instructing, and informing our youth ahead of time is always a better strategy than trying to catch it and correct it after the fact.

Pastors and youth leaders, if you plan on discussing things of this nature with young people in your charge, I recommend finding a good curriculum from a reputable publisher and sharing it with the parents in your church prior to teaching anything to their kids. I also encourage you to let your beliefs on casual sex, self-pleasure, pornography, and vanity be known at some point, perhaps once a year or at the commencement of classes. Let your families know that you will be sharing those biblical views as is appropriate throughout your time with their children, and that you encourage parents to do so on a regular and consistent basis as well. Invite them to talk through these issues with you so they have a biblical understanding of God's plan for sex. Impart to them the urgency and priority of instilling their kids with the essentials of biblical sexual integrity amid a world full of sexual propaganda.

THE LINK BETWEEN SEXUAL HARASSMENT AND PORNOGRAPHY

As I write this book, the media is blowing up about sexual harassment and the objectification of women in our culture. It's maddening—what did we expect would happen when we placed sex at the top of our priority lists? Hollywood wants to sell more movies, and the way to do that is more sex. A pharmaceutical company wants to increase their revenue, so they insert a sexy couple into their ad campaign. A sport league needs more attention and sponsorship, so cue the Budweiser girls, half-naked dancers, and every sexual innuendo possible during the commercial breaks. Sex sells; this we know.

I can't help but think of Shari Lewis and her song that never ends. This cycle of sexual abuse feels never-ending sometimes. We doubt ourselves and our beliefs because we stand out from the rest of the world.

Sex sells because it stimulates addictive chemical responses in the human brain. Here's a major news bulletin: sex was God's idea! He created sex so husbands and wives would continue to bond throughout the course of their marriage and create families together. Are we surprised that something God created for good, Satan has sickly twisted into something perverse that causes good people to fall into a never-ending cycle of sin, guilt, shame, remorse, and isolation? Sure, it feels good for a little while. Don't forget to tell your kids that, because the first few times they experience it, if they make that choice, it will absolutely feel good, and they will immediately write off your instruction as being "traditional and old-school, irrelevant to me in my enlightened and contemporary age." Give them all the full scoop, good and bad, and give it to them regularly.

Temptations are tempting because they usually feel good—for a little while. We think that it will always feel that good. It's important to discuss this with your teens often. This is how Satan hooks us. He's all about living in the moment, with no interest in the future of the person. God, on the other hand, has designed our lives with full knowledge that this life is short compared to all of eternity, which we will spend with Him in heaven. God is all about stability, constancy, absolutes, and long-terms. His design for sex between a husband and wife feels good forever because it produces all good things that *last.*

Adults—67 percent of males and 49 percent of females—are okay with pornography and agreed that viewing sexually explicit material is an acceptable way to express one's sexuality.[28] Studies also show, however, that viewing sexually explicit material has the power to distort our views on sex.[29] Could this be a contributing reason to the rise in sexual harassment in our modern culture? Men and women alike have been desensitized to the hypersexuality with which we've surrounded ourselves, until we are jolted back to reality when someone acts inappropriately to us, personally. The following is an excerpt from a study compiled by the Sexual Addiction and Compulsivity Task Force in 2012:

In 2009, Brown and L'Engle conducted a longitudinal study that confirmed a relationship between permissive sexual attitudes

---

28 J. S. Carroll, L. M. Padilla-Walker, L. J. Nelson, et al., "Generation XXX: Pornography Acceptance and Use among Emerging Adults," *Journal of Adolescent Research* 23, no. 1 (January 2008): 6; cited by Milton Diamond, "Pornography, Public Acceptance and Sex Related Crime: A Review," The Pacific Center for Sex and Society, http://www.hawaii.edu/PCSS/biblio/articles/2005to2009/2009-pornography-acceptance-crime.html (accessed May 18, 2018).

29 Jochen Peter, Patti M. Valkenburg, "Adolescents' Exposure to Sexually Explicit Internet Material and Notions of Women as Sex Objects: Assessing Causality and Underlying Process," *Journal of Communication* 59, issue 3 (September 2009): 425, https://academic.oup.com/joc/article/59/3/407/4098518 (accessed April 18, 2018).

and exposure to sexually explicit material. In addition, the authors also found a relationship between adolescent exposure to sexually explicit material and less progressive gender role attitudes for both males and females. For example, Brown and L'Engle's study indicated that male dominance and female submission are gender roles that are reinforced through sexually explicit material.

Beliefs of women as sex objects are defined by Peter and Valkenburg (2009) as "ideas about women that reduce them to their sexual appeal in terms of their outer appearance and their body (parts)" (p. 408). Peter and Valkenburg (2009) state that "such notions also entail a strong concern with women's sexual activities as a main criterion of their attractiveness and focus on women as sexual playthings that are eager to fulfill male sexual desires" (p. 408). Peter and Valkenburg (2007) published a study of Dutch adolescents (N = 745) that investigated the relationship between exposure to sexually explicit material and perceptions of women as sex objects. Their study found that increased exposure to sexually explicit material increased the likelihood that adolescents, regardless of gender, would view women as sex objects. In a later study designed to clarify these findings, Peter and Valkenburg (2009) determined that viewing women as sex objects was related to increased frequency in the consumption of sexually explicit material. It is unclear how adolescent females are impacted by viewing other females, and possibly even themselves, as sex objects. In short, these findings suggest that "adolescents' exposure to SEIM [Sexually Explicit Internet Material] was both a cause and a consequence of their beliefs that women are sex objects" (p. 425).[30]

---

30 Eric W. Owens, Richard J. Behun, Jill C. Manning, and Rory C. Reid, "The Impact of Internet Pornography on Adolescents: A Review of the Research," *Sexual Addiction and Compulsivity: The Journal of Treatment and Prevention* 19, no. 1–2 (April 2012): 99–122. DOI: 10.1080/10720162.2012.660431(accessed April 18, 2018).

PORNOGRAPHY AND MARRIAGE

Taking into consideration the facts laid out above and what I know about the divorce rates in America, I began looking into the effects of pornography and sex addiction on our marriages. According to a study done by the American Sociological Association in 2016, divorce rates doubled when couples began watching porn.[31] While watching pornography is associated with an increase in the probability of divorce for all married Americans, the increase was even greater for younger adults. In fact, the study found that the younger an adult was when he or she began watching pornography, the higher his or her probability of getting divorced before the next survey period. Younger Americans are more likely to view pornography more often than older Americans, and older Americans generally have more stable marriages, since they tend to be more mature, financially stable, and have more time invested in the relationship.

This study also gave some wonderful insight into the benefits of the Christian lifestyle:

> Beginning pornography use was also associated with a greater negative impact on the marriages of those who were less religious, which was measured by religious service attendance. For those who did not attend religious services every week or more, beginning pornography use was associated with an increase from 6 percent to 12 percent in the probability of getting divorced by the next survey. By contrast, those who attended

---

31 Samuel Perry, "Till Porn Do Us Part? Longitudinal Effects of Pornography Use on Divorce," American Sociological Association study (working paper, University of Oklahoma, 2016), cited by Elizabeth McCauley, "Beginning Pornography Use Associated with Increase in Probability of Divorce," American Sociological Association press release (2016), http://www.asanet.org/press-center/press-releases/beginning-pornography-use-associated-increase-probability-divorce (accessed April 20, 2018).

religious services at least weekly saw virtually no increase in
their probability of divorce upon starting to view pornography.
According to Perry, the fact that being more religious seemed
to lessen the negative influence of pornography use on marital
stability deviates from some previous research.[32]

Our bodies, much like our marriages and our families
(the procreation of children), are sacred in nature. They
are sanctified, holy, and blessed by God. When we fail to
acknowledge that fact, we blur the lines, and our focus is
drawn to superficialities of the body that change the way we
approach ourselves and others. Through sexual propaganda
and pornography, the body is often portrayed in an unrealistic way—in fact, it's grossly misrepresented. This leads
people to see their body as an object rather than an essential
part of their total makeup.

Buying into this view can lead to near worship and pursuit of the so-called perfect body, and when a person doesn't
match up, it then leads to self-loathing. I have a good friend
who confided in me once about her husband's sex addiction.
Although he was struggling with an addiction to sex, they
ended up facing a crisis they could never have imagined: he
didn't want to have sex with her. It all began with a little
online porn that escalated into aggressive sexual acts and
online affairs. When that didn't satisfy him, he resorted to
watching hard-core porn and masturbating. His wife woeful-
ly understood. Porn never had kids to deal with, had stress
at work, required snuggle time, or got a headache. She began
to blame herself for his sinful behavior.

32 McCauley, "Beginning Pornography Use."

The reason I share this is because this addiction escalates just like a drug addiction. There's no end to it until a person seeks treatment and the healing that only Christ can give. It ruins families, as we've seen in the above-mentioned statistics, and it demeans the sacred nature of intimacy and the human body. To exploit the human body is to exploit Him who is the light and the life of the world, dying for you and living within you.

MACHISMO

In preparation for our mission work in Latin America, our family was required to learn Spanish. After a year of preparation and nearly three years in the field, the five of us Ruesches are equivalent to one really good Spanish speaker. Now that we are back in the States, I find that there are many words I used in Spanish that actually express what I want to say better than the English vocabulary I've been fine-tuning my whole life. *Machismo* is one of those words. *Machismo* means that a man has an unusually high or exaggerated sense of masculinity. It implies an attitude that aggression, strength, sexual prowess, power, and control are the measure of someone's manliness. A man with machismo feels that having these traits entitles him to respect and obedience from men and women around him. This word also encompasses a belief in the right to dominate over and control women.

When it comes to teaching our youth about sexual integrity, I can't stress this enough: men, be man enough to teach your sons the value of human life. Women, be strong enough to assert yourselves as worthy of your son's absolute respect. Because of the sexually explicit culture we live in, because of the pornography industry, because as much as 60 percent of our youth are being raised in single-parent homes, we have to be aware of this weakness in the character development of our boys. Boys from single-parent homes are far more susceptible when it comes to developing this attitude toward others and toward women especially.

What we need is a balance. Our young men need to see the value in becoming men of God: strong in body as well as in mind and spirit. It's easy to think that little girls are the only ones who dream of a healthy marriage and family someday, but I can tell you from firsthand experience as I meet with students across the country and even around the world that boys want to be invited into the conversation. Men wanted to be daddies at one point in their lives. They drew pictures of a house with a mom and a dad, kids and a dog. God created them to leave their parents and attach themselves to their wives, to pass their names down to their sons, and to create a heritage of which their families would be proud for generations to come.

This is an innate desire of all men, whether they acknowledge it or not. Because of environmental influences such as divorce, rigorous work demands, and ignorance stemming from a lack of strong men in their own lives, many men no longer feel they have the right to work toward these things. When speaking with a guy who is recovering from a sex addiction, I was told that his life of casual, meaningless sex was a defense mechanism after the hurt of his divorce. He basically said, "I'm done trying to be an upstanding guy. I'm just going to do what works for me right now so that I don't ever have to commit to anyone and get hurt ever again." After many years, he realized the hurt he was causing himself and his kids, and he sought counseling and treatment. His story is powerful because, on a grander scale, this is what we've done to our boys who have grown into men and are seeking so much to find that healthy marriage. I was speaking at a teen camp retreat once, and afterward a very large and tough-looking football player came up to me with his whole group of buddies in tow and said, "I want to have the marriage you have someday."

Emphasize this to your teens: do not underestimate or underemotionalize anyone. God created us with a divine design and operating system. We are programmed to seek after a spouse and procreate. That doesn't have to be the *only* thing we do in this life, but a healthy dose of respect for it would go a long way. When we recognize and place importance on the benefits of marriage in the lives of our teens, they will grow up understanding the order that God created and the beauty that is found in each individual human life—so much so that they wouldn't dream of disrespecting it.

That's not too much to expect, is it?

In a nutshell, why are pornography and self-pleasure wrong?

- They defile our souls for which Jesus Christ atoned.

- They defile the value of marriage.

- They become addictive and habitual.

- A person becomes dependent on the rush of chemicals the body creates. (Contributing to the addiction! Often youth depend on this rush to help them deal with negative emotions, such as boredom, stress, loneliness, hurt, or anger.)

- They can escalate like any other addiction and cause extramarital affairs or sexual dissatisfaction within the marriage.

- They create unhealthy expectations for marriage.

CHAPTER 3

Discussion Questions

»   Sex was never meant to be the main focus of the body. It's an important part of the body because it supports or lends itself to what?

»   What is the greatest form of spiritual warfare? Why must our teens be aware of it?

»   There is significant research (and our own common sense) that proves pornography leads the human mind to think of women as sexual objects rather than human beings with tremendous value. Talk about the links between the pornography industry and sexual harassment and abuse in our culture.

»   Masturbation has long been seen as an acceptable way to stifle the temptation to engage in sexual acts outside of marriage. Why is this a lie? How does masturbation hurt the person in the long run?

» Who is more likely to suffer a divorce when viewing pornography, older couples or younger? Why is that? How can we come alongside the youth in our lives to help them protect their (future) marriages from the effects of pornography?

» Why is exploiting the human body an exploitation of Jesus Christ Himself?

Teens and Homosexuality

And I saw the beast and the kings of the earth with their armies gathered to make war against Him who was sitting on the horse and against His army.

REVELATION 19:19

A great battle is seething among us. A culture war is on-going between the media, movies, music, literature, public schools, and universities against Christians, the Church, and the inerrant Word of God. As this battle rages everywhere around us, we may find ourselves as simple, innocent by-standers, well-wishers with hopes of peace for the future.

But what happens when one side meets the other and the battleground at which the first sword is drawn is your child? or a family member? or someone in your congregation?

"Mom, Dad—I'm gay."

"Pastor, does God hate me because I'm attracted to guys *and* girls?"

"My best friend thinks she's a lesbian, and I don't know what to do."

What's our job, then, as the battle becomes personal for a parent, pastor, or youth leader?

At any time, we can access information about homosexuality and the homosexual lifestyle if we want to dig deeper or have a better understanding of all its complexities. Literature, Bible studies, and scientific research are just one Google search away. But when the battle is suddenly taking place in the heart, mind, and soul of someone we care about, we find ourselves on one side of the culture war—his or her side. The side of the person we're close to.

Our interest and concern become interpersonal rather than educational.

Truth be told, in this present time, most of us know someone who is gay or bisexual, and we seek to relate well with them. How is the prominence and openness of the gay lifestyle affecting our teens and their relationships with others? How can we come alongside them as they try to maneuver through this battleground and seek to find themselves in Christ rather than in the world?

The answer is right before us. When we lose our way, or when life gets confusing, we must step back and remind ourselves who we are. This battle is much less about sexuality and much more about identity.

I've always loved art. Drawing and writing books were my favorite things to do when I was a kid. The best time of year was always late August, when we got to go shopping for school supplies. The potential of a brand-new box of crayons still gets me excited, even now. I remember opening the box, and the smell would instantly spark my imagination as I began to see the things I'd create with it.

I was, therefore, very protective of my school supplies. I'd grab the shopping bag, and as soon as we got home, I'd get out that black permanent marker and write my name on every single thing. I didn't want anyone mistaking my stuff for theirs. In this same way, God places His name on us in our Baptism. We belong to Him, and He doesn't want anyone else stealing us away. Yet Satan is the ultimate thief. We know that he comes to steal, kill, and destroy, and he is doing that very well through the lies of homosexuality as he robs our youth of their identity and blurs the lines of their sexuality.

Throwing open the door on this will not happen overnight. Most likely, none of us will ever walk into a room full of teenagers and have this mind-blowing connection where we all just see ourselves through God's eyes and are changed. But don't judge what God is doing by the results you see. Ever. If there's one thing I've learned as a mom of teens and as a youth speaker, kids allow you to see only what they want you to see. Be patient and consistent. Quality conversation after quality conversation, after listening, after seeking them out, all with the intent of rolling up your sleeves and getting integrated into their lives—these things will make you a person they want to emulate. Every time they see Christ in you, they will be reminded of Christ in them.

The prodigal son was lost and then found himself again upon his return to his family. The child who believes him- or herself to be gay or bisexual needs to hear, "You are my son. You are my daughter. You are a treasured child of God before you are anything else." Even if children reject that, the goal of the Church is always to bring them back, always to remind them of who they are. The family, a microcosm of the Church, operates in the very same way. Forgiveness, love, and yes, Law too. We always yearn to pull the child back into the family. We continually show him or her what it looks like to be a child of God and a treasured member of the family of Christ, and nothing can ever change that.

COMMUNICATION

Here's something I think about a lot: it seems easier for these kids to identify as gay than it is for them to contend with the life, or the hand, they've been dealt. There are so many circumstantial and environmental challenges that make the twenty-first century unlike that of any before it. There's a breakdown in relationships like never before.

As I stated in chapter 1, if we aren't intentionally teaching our children God's ways, the world will have its way with our children. Unfortunately, opening the lines of communication with teens is not the easiest thing to do. Yet we must, as parents and youth leaders, make the effort.

When possible, start early. Talk to your children about everything and anything, and listen when they speak to you. (Even when it's about Minecraft or who's mad at whom because she didn't smile the right way.)

Establishing this trust and showing your children that they have your time earns respect. That respect develops into admiration, and that admiration helps to develop their character. Not only will they trust you, but they will want to be like you.

As is the case for a lot of us, though, you may be seeking to reach a young person who is already in the throes of a hard life and may or may not belong to you. In that case, approach that person with the same foundation. Find a way to connect, and then be ready to listen. Look for a way to integrate value into his or her life, and just be present. It begins with giving your time and sharing stories. These two things create a sense of empathy as well as the ability to see beyond the issues that lie on the surface and into the depths of another person's life. A genuine heart of love that flows first from Christ into us and then from us into the world is irreplaceable and incredibly healing. We, as parents and ministry workers, err on the side of love, Christ's love, with every teen who's placed before us, because of our understanding of Christ's unconditional love for us.

When my kids were young, I spent some time teaching in a Lutheran preschool and daycare center. Children are inherently generous with their love. First thing in the morning, we would gather on our circle-time rug and draw names to assign each person a task or responsibility for the day. Every child was so excited to draw names until everyone had a job. Their little eyes beamed as they proudly accepted positions such as handing out napkins for snack time, leading their friends to the lunchroom, or passing out blankets for an afternoon nap.

It feels good to take care of one another.

Working with teenagers, I see many of these same behaviors carried through from their younger years. When the opportunity is presented to help, include, or care for a peer, almost every student is willing—they just don't always know how to help. Hasn't that been true for all of us at different points in our lives? Establishing empathy through mutual stories and experiences is a stepping stone toward knowing how to help.

IDENTIFYING AS LGBTQIA (LESBIAN, GAY, BISEXUAL, TRANSGENDER, QUEER, INTERSEX, OR ASEXUAL)

It's not surprising to me in the least that as the relationships within the modern family become more disjointed, our kids are searching among themselves for meaningful relationships and stronger connections. As a result, many identify as bisexual or homosexual because they feel a stronger bond with a peer who has been there for them in a more meaningful way than anyone else in their life so far.

This is much more about connection and much less about sexuality.

Sex is the teenage interpretation of deep caring, gratitude for relationship, and hormones. Rather than fixing the root of the issue—the absence of meaningful relationship in the home—the culture uses homosexuality as a type of justification for the emptiness our youth are feeling. "You're not lonely; you're gay." "You're not different and unique; you're gay."

The irony is that they *are* different, and they *are* uniquely made (Psalm 139), but they won't feel like it until they feel they belong somewhere. There's power in numbers, and that's because none of us want to be alone. Remember that we were created to be relational people. Every person will forge strong ties somewhere, if not to their home or church family then to a family where they feel accepted, even if they know they are compromising their morals in the process. Love is such a powerful thing; as sinful human beings, we can justify almost anything to make sure we have it. I will say this, however: there's a big difference between justified love and true, unconditional love.

When I bring up the topic of homosexuality in a group setting or classroom, students immediately begin to share stories about a friend they have known their whole lives who just came out, or about a girl at school whose parents are going to disown her when they find out she's bisexual. These are people they love and with whom they are in relationship every day. They share a mutual empathy with one another that creates a bond between them. They care deeply about their friends because they are, for lack of better words, forced to be in relationship with one another for eight hours a day, five days a week! And that number is quite possibly more if you take into consideration their sports, clubs, and recreational time.

As adults, do we spend that amount of time with anyone? Especially our families, with whom God intended us to share our everyday lives? Past generations have never talked so openly about the homosexual lifestyle and integrated it within their communities. It existed, but it was hardly spoken of. With an increasing amount of young people identifying as lesbian, gay, bisexual, transgender, queer or questioning, intersex, or asexual (LGBTQIA), we are faced with the choice either to make it someone else's problem or, as I see it, to take the opportunity to model and teach them about their identity in Jesus, via our connecting empathy and consistent relationship.

When I talk with these people, I search to see past their perceived sexuality and into their stories, into their days, their situations, and their pain.

"I have a friend who is scared to tell her parents she's bisexual."

"Tell me about her life" would be my response. What is going on in her life that is making her feel that a bisexual relationship is the solution or part of the solution to her pain? I don't ask that right away, but I absolutely have it in mind.

When John said, "We love because He first loved us" (1 John 4:19), he gave us a foundational means to relate to one another. We invest in one another and patiently take the time necessary because human life is valuable. It's worth the investment.

THE IDENTITY OF THE FAMILY

One of the most important lessons I've learned in my life is one I learned from an incredible woman who served with me at my first pregnancy center. Upon my arrival, she told me, "We always tell our advocates and volunteers something very important: 'It's our job to love our clients and come alongside them, not to change them. That's God's job.'" I never forgot that, and I cling to those words even now. I like things to be wrapped up decent and in order. Probably like you, I am a doer; when I see something that needs to be fixed, I fix it. It can be incredibly frustrating when all we want is to "be the change" in someone else's life.

The problem is that we often have in mind this valiant moment of success rather than the hit-and-miss baby steps it takes to get there. We often lack the faith or trust that God will work His grace and mercy in the situation. But this is key: God, our Father and Creator, knows every single little thing that's going on with every single one of us. Psalm 139 says that He knew everything we would say and do—good, bad, and ugly—before even a word was on our lips, and He still deemed us worthy to create. Who am I, then, to commandeer God's plans and try to take over the work He's doing in other people's lives through the Holy Spirit? We exist to be in relationship with God and with one another in order that others might be in relationship with Him as well. This happens first by means of our Baptism, in which we took on our Father's name; next through His Word, by which the Holy Spirit creates faith in us; and finally in Holy Communion, with which He cleanses us with the body and blood of His Son. We are left standing renewed, forgiven, and set back on our feet to face a new day. I have nothing to offer anyone that even comes close to that. Instead, I pray for the humility of my Lord, which puts me back into my place as a sister to all in Christ, instead of trying to be the Father, who's already got the (spiritual) family situation in hand.

Having said that, I want to make sure that you know that the job of the Christian is certainly not just to sit back and hold the "I Heart Jesus" sign either. We should have strong convictions about teaching God's Word to the world and especially to our children. And that's okay; in fact, it's good. You'll get a few things right, and some things wrong too, as you speak up and learn how to convey the truth of God's Word to a hurting world.

We don't have to be perfect or well-rehearsed or even professionals. We just need to know what God says about sex and relationships, and then we need to take that information and bring it to others by means of relationships, starting with our own families first. I have sat with and walked alongside far too many teens struggling with homosexuality to buy into the lie that there aren't many serious and varying factors contributing to a rise in this lifestyle. I feel we do a grave disservice to those kids carrying such burdens when we pretend that they are brave and empowered rather than suffering greatly.

Everyone out there is trying to "find themselves." Searching for purpose and identity is the trend of our time. It is the job and the God-given privilege of parents, of moms and dads, to teach their children who they are, what their identity is, and first and foremost, from whom it comes.

Many years ago, I was leading a women's Bible study retreat where I was asked to speak on who God is. As part of the retreat, the ladies prepared a wonderful little card that had the names and characteristics of God written on it. I carried that card around with me for years afterward, until it was so beat up that I had to throw it away. It was invaluable to me, because it took only one quick glance to remind me of my heritage and of who my Father is. One day some time ago, when I was feeling particularly defeated, I got into my car and caught sight of that card. I remember hearing in my head whatever movie character said, "Do you know who my father is?" I laughed out loud at my own ridiculous sense of humor, but nevertheless I cataloged that moment in my mind. Do we know who our Father is? Do we speak with Him during the day as we come face-to-face with sin, evil, and the devil himself? I like to picture God standing with me, guiding me and strengthening me against Satan's arrows and the challenges that I inevitably encounter in my life.

This is what we can take to heart about the identity of our God, our Father, in whom we find our identity:

He tells us that He is Elohim. *Elohim* is a Hebrew word that is plural in form. It refers to the Father, Son, and Holy Spirit. The plurality of this name is so important that God identifies Himself this way to us right away in Genesis 1:1: "In the beginning, God [Elohim] created the heavens and the earth." What does this mean? It means that all of God was present and are accountable for all creation. For example, my family name is Ruesch. We are one family but five persons. Elohim is God in three persons. It is God's name that He uses to associate Himself with the creation of the world and everything in it. Perhaps this isn't the greatest analogy, but my hope is that you might understand the concept a little better. *Elohim* is important to us because in this name, God tells us that He is triune and that He is our Creator. Elohim, our Creator.

In due order, when Moses asked God what name he should give to the Israelites if they asked who sent him, God told him, "Yahweh," or "I AM WHO I AM" (Exodus 3:14): the Self-Existing, Uncreated One. We are human beings, but God is simply Being, meaning that He had no beginning and will have no end. The name *Yahweh* allows us to see the big picture, so to speak; in it, we catch a glimpse of how great our God is and the timeless power He holds. This is of the greatest comfort when Satan's schemes bind us into situations that leave us feeling hopeless. There is nothing new under the sun, and God has seen it all. He always has a way, even when we cannot fathom otherwise. Our minds are so incapable compared to the vast knowledge of God. Yahweh, I AM WHO I AM.

The Hebrew name *Adonai* in English translates to "my Master." It describes for us the lordship of God over us all as individuals. In Hebrew, *Adon* means not only "master" but also "steward, overseer, or lord." Jesus said in Romans 6:16 that the one whom you obey is your lord. If He is not Lord of everything, He is not Lord of anything. We cannot claim God as our Lord if we do not seek to obey Him. He is either Adonai, our Master, or He is not. If He is not, then we presently have the wrath of God still abiding in us. Oh, the gravity of repentance! God, Adonai, reminds us that sin is not something He takes lightly or overlooks. It needs to be rectified before we can come into His holy presence. Adonai created us for relationship and wants us close to Him. It was crucial that He send His Son to accept in our stead the wrath that we deserve, thus allowing us to come freely to our Master and Overseer with all that we need to share with Him. Adonai, our Master.

SCRIPTURE CONNECTION

Do you not know that if you present yourselves to anyone as obedient slaves, you are slaves of the one whom you obey, either of sin, which leads to death, or of obedience, which leads to righteousness? (Romans 6:16)

Finally, let's look at the name of God that refers to His giving nature: *Yahweh Yireh* (sometimes written as *Jehovah Jireh*), the provider, the salvation for all. The name *Yahweh Yireh* comes from the story of Abraham and the sacrifice of Isaac. After God provided the ram for the sacrifice in place of Isaac, "Abraham called the name of that place, 'the LORD will provide'" (Genesis 22:14). *Yahweh Yireh* is the provision plan in the sacrifice of the Lamb, Jesus Christ, for the sins of His children. He provided for us Jesus Christ so we could be restored into right relationship with God. He supplied the restoration that was necessary because of our sinfulness, which separated us from Him. Yahweh Yireh, our provision.

God has many other names that He reveals to us throughout Scripture. Looking them up and studying Him is even better than taking those Myers-Briggs personality tests. The many facets of God are endless, compelling us to know Him more and more. As we better understand who He is, we better understand ourselves and our place in this world too.

For the sake of practical application, consider this example. My husband, as the head of our home and father to our three children, is always saying such things: "Ruesches do for others before themselves," "Ruesches go to church on Sunday mornings," and "In every instance, listen; show humility and love first." He leads us in devotions and prayer before bedtime and meals. All of these things, big and small, contribute to the identity of the child. Parents and grandparents are leaders, whether they want to be or not. Your children have been soaking in your every action and move since before they were born. Even in the womb, babies are conscious of the climate of their environment; they sense what is being thought, said, felt, or done all around them.

It's up to the parents to create an environment of identity within the home. It's the work of the Church to share the love of Christ and the forgiveness of sins. When young people are searching to find themselves, God gives us our families, both at home and in the Church, to remind us who we are.

If the Church's job is to reflect the love of God the Father to His children, then the family's job, being a microcosm of the Church, is to reflect that love to their children as well. If this is missing in some way, if a child is struggling or hurting or identifying as something other than who God created him or her to be, then what does that child need to be shown above all else? The love of God the Father.

THE BIBLE, OUR OPERATIONS MANUAL

The Bible, the Word that was made flesh in the coming of Christ, determines our worldview and encompasses our identity. It's much easier to explain why I believe what

I believe when I first understand why I believe it. So, when people say to me, "What do you think about gay marriage?" I can fall back on my general operations manual, the Bible, and know that God created marriage to be between a man and woman; anything outside that boundary is sinful, harmful to the individual and to others. (Again, remember that contrary to what we've all heard, God gives us boundaries because He knew that whatever He created to be awesome and amazing, Satan would distort into something dangerous and destructive.)

The following verses show us, directly, that homosexuality is a sin in the eyes of God and is destructive to our relationship with Him, ourselves, and others. Men were not created to have sexual interactions with men, nor women with women.

> Do you not know that the unrighteous will not inherit the kingdom of God? Do not be deceived: neither the sexually immoral, nor idolaters, nor adulterers, nor men who practice homosexuality, nor thieves, nor the greedy, nor drunkards, nor revilers, nor swindlers will inherit the kingdom of God. (1 Corinthians 6:9–10)

> Now the works of the flesh are evident: sexual immorality, impurity, sensuality, idolatry, sorcery, enmity, strife, jealousy, fits of anger, rivalries, dissensions, divisions, envy, drunkenness, orgies, and things like these. I warn you, as I warned you before, that those who do such things will not inherit the kingdom of God. (Galatians 5:19–21)

Now we know that the law is good, if one uses it
lawfully, understanding this, that the law is not laid
down for the just but for the lawless and disobedient,
for the ungodly and sinners, for the unholy and
profane, for those who strike their fathers and
mothers, for murderers, the sexually immoral,
men who practice homosexuality, enslavers, liars,
perjurers, and whatever else is contrary to sound
doctrine, in accordance with the gospel of the glory
of the blessed God with which I have been entrusted.
(1 Timothy 1:8–11)

God Himself says that homosexuality is a sin. I point
this out because I'm often confronted with the statement,
"Nowhere in the Bible does it say that homosexuality is a
sin." Well, there you go. Here are several verses that can be
pointed out. (In fact, I recommend doing an in-depth Bible
study on these three passages.) But God doesn't stop there:
He continually separates the acts of the flesh from the acts
of the spirit, dividing the person into two beings—the sinner
and the saint. God has had to make some strong provisions
in order to keep us safe from the desires of the flesh, the
sexual immoralities, of this world.

And those who belong to Christ Jesus have crucified
the flesh with its passions and desires. If we live by
the Spirit, let us also keep in step with the Spirit.
(Galatians 5:24–25)

For all have sinned and fall short of the glory of God.
(Romans 3:23)

> Those who live according to the flesh set their minds on the things of the flesh, but those who live according to the Spirit set their minds on the things of the Spirit. (Romans 8:5)

We are all susceptible to different types of sin, and not one of us is given to the exact same sins as another. Every sin corrupts, but sexual immorality affects us in a way that other sins do not. It's a sin that wraps around and pulls down not just the body but also the heart, mind, and spirit with it. It is an intimate sin against the body, holistically. Not every sin is like that. Paul says plainly in 1 Corinthians 6:18 that "every other sin a person commits is outside the body, but the sexually immoral person sins against his own body."

Dr. John Kleinig, in his presentation "The Beauty of Chastity," says the following most profound statement:

> This argument for chastity both before marriage and in marriage has as its foundation the conviction that sex, though obviously physical, is also a deeply personal matter. For better or worse, it touches and affects me in my very self. It has as much, if not more, to do with my mind than with my body. It affects what I think, how I feel and what grips my imagination. It has, in fact, more to do with my soul, my sense of self, me as a whole person rather than me as a man. Thus if sex is not properly personalized, it can depersonalize those who engage in it.[33]

---

33 John W Kleinig, "The Beauty of Chastity," presentation given at a Doxology Insight Conference (St. Louis, MO: August 12–13, 2015), p. 2, http://www.johnkleinig.com/files/1514/4210/8671/Beauty_of_chastity.pdf (accessed April 20, 2018).

COEXISTING

Christian camaraderie cannot be confused with tolerance. So often, we hear this word being thrown around and misused. If we disagree with the transgender lifestyle, we are intolerant. If we walk alongside feminists in a pro-choice parade, we are marked as brave and tolerant people.

The word itself literally means to tolerate something that is disagreeable. The tremendous irony here is that I've met very few homosexuals who will say they chose to live this way. In actuality, very many of them are tolerating this burden themselves. They've been lied to by the great crafter of deception and made to believe that there is no other way. At the end of the day, I find great comfort in the knowledge that, as I stated before, it's not my job to change anyone. I can't.

However, I can love anyone, no matter how much I disagree or struggle with their decisions. Jesus Christ Himself loved each of us so much that He gave His life for us. To follow in His footsteps and share His love is to share the hope of healing and peace with all those who suffer.

Although it's not the most popular concept in modern Christianity, to embrace the reality of sin and receive the gift of forgiveness is the most healing and liberating act a human being can experience. Love at its core is mercy.

I can love a cute puppy or a beautiful rose bush in bloom, but that love pales in comparison to my mother or father pulling me close and saying, "I love you; I forgive you," after I've done something terribly wrong. Their mercy sparks a depth of love within me that compares only to the mercy God shows us through the most loving act of all time: putting His own Son to death so I can stand before Him with a clean slate. I cower behind the beaten body of Christ each time I come before Him in repentance for my sins.

God is the Creator of all things, the Father to the fatherless, and the Light to the empty and the lost. He knows every hair on our heads and works all things for the good of those who love Him. He is invested in every detail of our lives, no matter how hopeless those details may seem to us.

Our stories are His stories, and He gives them to us so that we might bring them to one another as an encouragement and testimony of the great work He does in our lives.

BEING COURTEOUS NEVER GETS OLD

There's something really important we need to understand when it comes to homosexuality within our society and how we relate to it as Christians. My stance on this is very simple.

I don't have to agree with you to be courteous to you, and whether or not you're courteous to me doesn't change that. A person with a confrontational attitude may challenge my maturity and self-discipline, but I reserve the right to disengage freely from the situation if things go awry. However, if under any circumstances a person's legal or moral rights are at stake and danger is imminent, the authorities need to be contacted immediately.

I have a friend who is a brilliant actor, singer, and all-around-theatre kind of guy. When he was a teenager, he would often come to our house after school and hang out with our kids, talk, and share his music with me. One day, after school, I got a text from him saying that he had a hard day and wasn't coming over. Wanting to make sure he was all right and knowing he'd be hesitant to share, I engaged him in a texting conversation about my own joys and struggles of the day in order to relate and signify that I trusted him enough to open up to him and, therefore, he could trust me as well.

That worked.

It didn't take long before he showed up at my door, looking defeated and hurt. Possessing a more effeminate disposition than most of the other guys at his school, he was often teased and picked on by a few specific individuals. That day, they had cornered him at the end of the hallway and harassed him into tears. Thankfully, a friend of his saw what was happening and alerted a teacher. No physical harm was done, but emotionally, my friend was wounded and in a lot of pain. This incident was brought to the attention of the school authorities and parents, and in the end, the offenders were adequately disciplined for their poor choices.

On the opposite side of the coin, I myself have been verbally assaulted by members of the gay community for many and varying reasons, and without any prompting on my part. These kinds of actions are destructive and hurtful no matter who you are.

My point in sharing these stories is to show that possessing good character and courtesy goes both ways. It applies to every situation and every person. Treat others as you would like to be treated. I have amazing friends from all over the world and from different walks of life. Many of them don't agree with me on everything I believe, and vice versa. We still enjoy being in a room together; we even have conversations about the things we disagree on, and we still choose to get together again!

I can stand back and say with full humility, "It's not all about me"—and it's not all about you either.

The world is full of people. Everywhere you go, with the exception of your favorite cabin in the woods or an intentional solo moment stolen away, we are forced to live in community with those around us. It doesn't matter how much we pretend that our actions don't affect others; they always have, and they always will.

A minor but vocal population on the extreme sides of the liberal-to-conservative spectrum tends to turn the majority of us away from living out this fundamental, societal cornerstone. Fanatical leftists and rightists cover the news, radio, and especially social media with messages that urge us to place our focus and beliefs within ourselves. Self-empowerment, following your heart, and focus on you—these are common messages we hear that actually contradict the truth of what it takes to live peaceably with those around us.

---

em·pow·er[34]
verb
to give (someone) the authority or power to do something. to make (someone) stronger and more confident, especially in controlling their life and claiming their rights

---

What good is a sense of empowerment if it's solely for personal gain? Isn't empowerment intrinsically based on the principle that we become empowered in order that we may empower others? And if I follow my heart, doesn't it always lead me to follow my own desires rather than the needs of others and the will of God? Finally, approaching life with a

---

34 Adapted from "Empower," Merriam-Webster.com, https://www.merriam-webster. com/dictionary/empower (accessed April 20, 2018).

"do what's best for me" attitude will most certainly cause me to delve more deeply into myself.

The only way out for a lonely, individualistic culture is by flinging the doors to the world wide open and going back to the way our Creator intended us to be: focused outside of ourselves and more deeply in relationship with God the Father.

Don't know where to start? As a rule of thumb, when tempted to think that the world owes you something, find someone to serve. It happens to us all from time to time—the self-loathing. It manifests in being cruel and critical of other people's lives and choices. It's a prideful thing, really. Satan has it in mind that when we spend our time serving ourselves, it will separate us from those God has placed in our lives to support us, teach us, and love us.

By serving others, we defeat Satan's intentions in every way. We willingly and intentionally place ourselves in the eye of God's love and relationship, and together we are reminded that it's always been all about Him. Let us never forget that we are His beloved children.

CHAPTER 4

Discussion Questions

» What forces make us reluctant to speak openly about homosexuality? What should we be saying? How are we called to act toward homosexuals?

» What circumstances cause youth to be drawn to the LGBTQIA community?

» How can you, in your vocation as pastor, youth leader, parent, teacher, and all other vocations, help create a culture of families whose members know and embrace their identity in Christ? How does each member know and embrace their place within the family?

CHAPTER 5

What Is True Love?

Love as we currently see it in our culture is shallow and superficial. It's a complete letdown.

What makes love "true"? This is the question on every teenager's mind—on everyone's mind at different points in our lives, really.

"How will I know he or she is the one?"

I remember taking quizzes in magazines as a kid, making lists of the qualities I liked in boys and placing wishes under my pillow just in case that old wives' tale was true and I'd dream of my future husband that night. (Sidenote: My lists of attributes usually included that "he must have good hair, wear nice clothes, and have blue sparkly eyes.")

If only it was that simple!

It's completely normal and completely okay to have little idiosyncrasies we look for in the opposite sex, but it can't be the main focus. To further my point, we all know that you can be a real jerk and still have sparkly eyes, good hair, and nice clothes. Right?

If I'm going to spend the rest of my life with someone, create brand-new people with this person, and probably face some of life's greatest pains and joys with him, I'm definitely looking to bypass the superficial characteristics and find out what makes that person tick. And he should feel the same about me.

True love is sacrificial above all things. It puts the other person first and lays down its life for its loved ones. Of whom does that remind you? Jesus Christ, of course. It's tempting to look at love like a revolving door, as something we take a spin through to see if it works.

It's actually more accurate to picture true love like the little towers we built when we were kids, carefully setting blocks in support of more blocks. Who knew we were preparing for our future marriages at the age of three? True love, the way God intended it, isn't as complicated as the world has made it. It's actually pretty simple. Following along the lines of child's play, we all remember this little tune: "First comes love, then comes marriage, then comes the baby in the baby carriage." I'm going to amend that by making sure Jesus is the strong base that holds this tower up, because *this* is what true love is meant to look like:

Really easy, right? It's not possible to love someone else, truly, until we first wrap our brains around God the Father's absolute love for us. His love stirred Him so deeply that He had to create a redemption plan for our lives so He wouldn't lose us.

The blocks must stack from there. If we never find romantic love with another human being, we still have Jesus.

If a marriage doesn't work out, a spouse passes away, or someone simply chooses not to marry, we still have Jesus.

If a couple finds themselves facing difficulties with their children, infertility, or the loss of a child, they still have the tremendous love of Jesus.

Take Jesus out of any of those scenarios, however, and we're left empty, begging others for answers and scraps of their love instead. This is the cheap love we're seeing all throughout our culture today. God never intended His children to beg for love. He says that we are sons and daughters of the King of kings. Not beggars desperate for whatever bone the world can throw us. As His children, we are more important and valuable to this world than anything else He's created. His love is liberally and freely given to us all.

In Psalm 139, God tells us exactly how He feels about us so we'll never doubt His love and intentions for our lives. I tried to pull just a couple verses to prove my point, but the entire psalm, every single verse, is so powerful that I couldn't pick just one. Here are verses 1–18 for you to soak in:

> O Lord, You have searched me and known me!
> You know when I sit down and when I rise up;
>   You discern my thoughts from afar.
> You search out my path and my lying down
>   and are acquainted with all my ways.
> Even before a word is on my tongue,
>   behold, O Lord, You know it altogether.
> You hem me in, behind and before,
>   and lay Your hand upon me.
> Such knowledge is too wonderful for me;
>   it is high; I cannot attain it.

Where shall I go from Your Spirit?
    Or where shall I flee from Your presence?
If I ascend to heaven, You are there!
    If I make my bed in Sheol, You are there!
If I take the wings of the morning
    and dwell in the uttermost parts of the sea,
even there Your hand shall lead me,
    and Your right hand shall hold me.
If I say, "Surely the darkness shall cover me,
    and the light about me be night,"
even the darkness is not dark to You;
    the night is bright as the day,
        for darkness is as light with You.

For You formed my inward parts;
    You knitted me together in my mother's womb.
I praise You, for I am fearfully and wonderfully made.
Wonderful are Your works;
    my soul knows it very well.
My frame was not hidden from You,
when I was being made in secret,
    intricately woven in the depths of the earth.
Your eyes saw my unformed substance;
in Your book were written, every one of them,
    the days that were formed for me,
        when as yet there was none of them.

How precious to me are Your thoughts, O God!
    How vast is the sum of them!
If I would count them, they are more than the sand.
    I awake, and I am still with You.

WHAT DOES TRUE LOVE LOOK LIKE?

> But the fruit of the Spirit is love, joy, peace, patience, kindness, goodness, faithfulness, gentleness, self-control; against such things there is no law. (Galatians 5:22–23)

The words "in Christ" are used quite a bit in Christian circles. I will often end a letter with those words or offer them in conjunction with a blessing of some sort: "Peace in Christ" or "All my love in Christ."

Saying those words as a Christian means that we understand that we're carrying Christ with us everywhere we go. That knowledge affects how we treat and relate to others as well as how we relate to ourselves. The Holy Spirit lives within us, guiding us and producing the good fruit that comes as a result of our faith in Him. The fruit of the Spirit is a litmus test, of sorts, for gauging whether your relationship is healthy for you and your significant other and pleasing to God.

Is there sacrificial love, joy in the midst of all other feelings, peace that passes all understanding?

Is there a mutual patience, kindness, and goodness between you?

Are you seeking to be faithful to God, first and foremost, and faithful to each other?

Do you approach each other with gentleness and self-control?

That's not to say that every God-pleasing relationship will always encompass all of these things, because we are sinful human beings after all, but it should be the goal of every relationship to be made up of these behaviors. The

Holy Spirit produces only good and loving things. If the Holy Spirit dwells within you and your boyfriend, girlfriend, or spouse, this good fruit will be evident.

In Galatians, Paul provides a contrast by describing the desires of the flesh before the fruit of the Spirit. This side of heaven, we are constantly struggling with two people at once: the old Adam, or the flesh, who seeks to fulfill the sinful, fallen desires of this world; and the new Adam, who seeks to drown those desires, cast them away, and live according to the Spirit.

Paul writes:

> But I say, walk by the Spirit, and you will not gratify the desires of the flesh. For the desires of the flesh are against the Spirit, and the desires of the Spirit are against the flesh, for these are opposed to each other, to keep you from doing the things you want to do. But if you are led by the Spirit, you are not under the law. Now the works of the flesh are evident: sexual immorality, impurity, sensuality, idolatry, sorcery, enmity, strife, jealousy, fits of anger, rivalries, dissensions, divisions, envy, drunkenness, orgies, and things like these. I warn you, as I warned you before, that those who do such things will not inherit the kingdom of God. (Galatians 5:16–21)

This, too, is a litmus test for your relationships. Are you following the desires of the flesh or the desires of the Spirit? Sometimes, when we are so immersed in the world we live in, it's hard to tell. The wrong can seem right because it's socially accepted, and the right can seem wrong because it's socially unaccepted. But we know that the ways of the world are not God's ways. Clear teaching and distinction challenge the mentality of the world with the logic of the truth of God.

Think about the rate at which our youth are absorbing the secular influences around them. As those who have been charged to mentor them, teach them, and care for their spiritual and bodily needs, we have to up our game. One chat a year about relationships and sex must be reconfigured into daily conversations and working to equip our congregational families.

Let me say now that it should never be assumed that kids know they shouldn't be having sex outside of marriage. They do not know that. It is impossible for me to count how many girls I've sat next to in pregnancy centers, clinics, and schools who have said, "Nobody told me."

Nobody told me not to have sex.

Nobody told me I would get a sexually transmitted infection.

Nobody told me I would hate myself.

Nobody told me I'd be a mom or a dad.

Nobody told me I'd be waiting my turn in an abortion clinic.

I have met fourteen-, fifteen-, sixteen-, and seventeen-year-olds who didn't understand how they got pregnant or got a girl pregnant. They knew they'd had sex, but that was as far as their understanding went. We assume, because this was taught to us in the eighties, nineties, and before, that this is taught to today's youth. It's not. I was appalled when I started asking my local public school districts, and Christian schools especially, what their sexual integrity programs were, only to find out that none of them had a specific and intentional curriculum they taught their students. I'd love to hear back from you, by the way, if you should decide to follow my lead and start asking what your local educational institutions are doing!

The shocking reality is that today's youth are learning about love, sex, and relationships first and foremost from the media: movies, music, YouTube, and television. They are play-acting what they see. When we recognize that, it's much easier to understand why so many of today's youth struggle to find meaningful relationships and why true love has become more like pie in the sky than a fairly straightforward and obtainable gift of God. Even the actors they are patterning their lives after know there's more to love than the fiction they portray in their shows. We have to be the ones who tell these kids the truth so they'll never have to say, "Nobody told me," ever again.

Paul says in Galatians 5:19 that the works of the flesh are evident. They are obvious when you're looking for them. Relationships produce works of the flesh in the following ways:

- Sexual immorality (generally the term used for all unlawful sexual intercourse; it includes adultery, prostitution, sexual relations between unmarried individuals, homosexuality, and bestiality)

- Impure thoughts or actions pertaining to yourself or others

- Sensuality or lust, whether within your mind or by causing someone else to lust after you

- Idolatry of earthly things

- Sorcery (participating or interacting with witchcraft, devil spirits, and evil forces)

Does your relationship seem always to be caught up in enmity, strife, jealousy, fits of anger, rivalries, dissensions, divisions, envy, drunkenness, orgies, and things of this nature? If so, then understand that the Holy Spirit cannot produce those things. God is the embodiment of true love. These things come from our sinful nature, and Satan uses them to separate us from God because he knows that when we are separated, we are alone and weak. But in Christ and with other believers, we are unified and unbreakable.

> A great visual learning tool to incorporate with your youth is to bind thirty pencils together with a rubber band. Ask them to try and break it in half. It's impossible! Now, take one of the pencils away from the rest of the group and ask them to try to break the isolated pencil. Much easier to do, isn't it? Together, we are strong; alone, we are weakened.

THE DANGLING CARROT

My daughter Bella loves horses. I, however, know nothing about them, and if I'm being honest, I'm a little bit afraid of them. When our family was serving as missionaries on the island of Puerto Rico, Bella and I had the opportunity to volunteer together at a local farm, taking care of their horses. I remember one particular morning; the sun was warm on our faces as we drove, and I was soaking up every minute of listening to her explain to me the intricacies and responsibilities that the owners had requested of us that particular day. I loved that she had something to share with me, and she loved that it was her, not I, who was the authority on a topic for a change.

Watching her work with one particularly stubborn horse made me laugh and think of an old comic strip I once saw. A farmer was hanging a carrot in front of his horse, which I imagine was acting similarly to the one standing before Bella. Both horses had in mind what they wanted to do, and neither of them was interested in what their caretakers' desires were for them. In the same way that Bella was trying to lead her horse to the grazing field with a treat in hand, the farmer was trying to lead his horse to an orchard full of juicy apples by means of a dangling carrot. Neither of the horses could see the intentions that were laid out before them. They saw only what was in front of them at the moment. The punch line was something pretty mundane, but I found a greater paradigm in it. Aren't we just like those horses when it comes to our relationships? We're often so focused on what feels good at the moment that we cease to realize we're surrounded by God's very best intentions. Our desires of the flesh make us stubborn and blind us from seeing the riches and freedom we have before us in Christ.

Be not distracted by the dangling carrot, the treat in front of your eyes.

The only true love is God's love. His love for us has to be the foundational block on which we build and are established. Without it, we can only do our best to play the part, like the actors in the movies we watch.

> Trust in the LORD with all your heart,
>   and do not lean on your own understanding.
> In all your ways acknowledge Him,
>   and He will make straight your paths.
> Be not wise in your own eyes;
>   fear the LORD, and turn away from evil.
> It will be healing to your flesh
>   and refreshment to your bones. (Proverbs 3:5–9)

CHAPTER 5

Discussion Questions

» How does Jesus affect our understanding of love?

» How does Psalm 139 describe the Father's love for us?

» Think about the youth you know and with whom you interact. Do they see love as something of substance or just a "dangling carrot"?

» What are the distractions that act as dangling carrots for our youth?

Christian Dating

THE GENERAL OPERATING SYSTEM

Take a moment and think. Do you know a couple, from your past or present, who just rocked at this whole family thing? They were amazing. Their kids were well-groomed and grounded, they had a nice house, and they had dinner on the table at six o'clock sharp every night. They came to church and sat in the same pew every week. Their family was the first to greet you or to volunteer to help with the monthly mission outreach.

What was it about their lives that makes you remember them now? Was it their respect for one another? their happy disposition? Or did they have something you felt you were missing?

Consequently, do you know a family, past or present, who always seem to be struggling? Maybe you feel like you're that family. Always in a rush, the kids' clothes don't match, the cat may or may not have peed on the husband's shoes before church, and their van was seen smoking in the parking lot of the bank. (These are all real-life examples given on behalf of the Ruesch family this week, by the way.)

What is it about their lives that makes you remember them? I'm willing to bet that empathy played a role in that memory. Perhaps there was a moment when you connected with them in their struggles because you could relate in some way.

We all compare ourselves to others who appear to be succeeding or failing, and we notice different characteristics in everyone we meet. Some we strive to emulate, and from some we strive to be as different as possible. The truth is that when it comes to parenting, everyone struggles. What works for one family doesn't necessarily work for another, and as we've spoken of already, we are sinners raising sinners.

The good news is that not one of us has to do it alone. God is always a step ahead of us, and He accommodates our weaknesses by giving us a community of support, so that together we all share in raising the child.

Somewhere along the way, preferably in the very beginning of their child's life, Mom and Dad, the cochairs of the family and each with very different responsibilities, will establish their general operating system, or GOS. The GOS will be the code of behavior or the rules of conduct for the family.

More important, this GOS serves as the moral compass for the rest of their lives. It helps determine who is in their community of support, how they approach challenges, and by which means life lessons are taught to their children.

Serving for many years now in Christian nonprofit ministries, schools, pregnancy centers, and churches, I can tell you that an organization is a mess without its GOS. In fact, anyone who knows me can attest that it's something I harp on all the time. In order to ensure success, in your home life or in any field of work or ministry, you must have a standard by which you operate. When a situation arises or your organization is falling apart, you don't abandon the job—you go back to your GOS, figure out where you've failed, refine it, and pick back up again.

Every one of us has adopted a system such as this that we use to dictate the daily events of our lives—and often we don't even realize it! One family adopts quietness, reflectiveness, and solitude as a way to think and process, while another family speaks loudly and processes verbally with one another until a solution is reached. Some people handle stress by drinking alcohol, while others hit the gym and physically pound it out. Sadly, when we try to do everything by ourselves, we end up with a hodgepodge of ideals that sounded good in the moment but don't necessarily go together. We're left feeling unsure about what our beliefs really are, and we punt every time a question of importance comes our way.

I once had a conversation with a minister who told me that when asked about sex at a youth gathering of approximately seventy students, he changed the subject because he didn't know what to say. He felt terrible after the fact because he knew that he had missed an extraordinary opportunity to speak truth to those kids. We began meeting regularly, and he developed a GOS so he would never let those kids down like that again.

A general operating system comprises three main parts: the operations manual, the mission statement, and the standards of procedure.

As Christians, our operations manual is the Bible. The Bible is our go-to at all times; there is no circumstance in which it isn't relevant to us anymore, not today and not at any time in history. In the Book of Ecclesiastes, Solomon says, "There is nothing new under the sun" (1:9). The Word of God is the same yesterday, today, and tomorrow. Everything we need to form our GOS is right there in Holy Scripture.

After the Bible, the mission statement and the standards of procedure (SOP) are the most important tools for daily operations. Every decision you make as the leader of an organization has to fall in line with those two things. When serving in nonprofit pregnancy center ministry, I read those documents daily, and sometimes more often. I needed to remember exactly who our mission statement said we were and how our standards of procedure said we did things. Inevitably, there were times when I would forget and go off on my own. I had people in my life, accountability partners, who would tell me that I'd gotten off track and needed to bring myself back in line with our mission statement so I could follow the standards of procedure.

Are you following so far? Can you see a connection yet between the general operating system and dating? Let's continue!

THE MISSION STATEMENT

We have established that there's a general operating system that determines how we live our lives: being a Christian. Within that system, we have an operations manual that tells us how we were created to live that life: the Bible.

Next, we have a mission statement. The mission statement sets the intentions of the organization and encompasses every area of importance or service. If we're applying the mission statement to the family (home or congregation), it would look something like this:

> As the Ruesch family, we seek to hold true to the inerrant Word of God before all else. We share the love of Christ with our

neighbor and defend all human life at every stage, honoring our Lord's sacrifice by striving to be good stewards of all He has provided us.

This mission statement then becomes our identity at a glance. In a few concise and powerful words, I am reminded what I'm all about. Even better, my kids, who are still maturing and growing and searching for answers, know what they are all about and from where it is that they come.

When there's conflict or division among us, we can come back to that mission statement and view our actions right alongside those words for comparison. Why do we hold true to the inerrant Word of God before all else? Because as sinners, we will try to justify our actions and behaviors by the world's standards rather than God's. Yes, we will. Every time.

For example, when teens want to disobey their parents and go to a party behind their backs, their friends may help them justify that decision in a hundred different ways. If their friends aren't around, they can always depend on their own emotions and logic to seal the deal. Been there, done that a few times in my life.

However, if I've been intentionally taught to fall back on my mission statement, which quickly reminds me who I am in Christ, I have a perspective that makes me accountable and gives me something much more concrete than emotions. It gives me doctrine. Bam. I am stronger, because I've got a great tool that I will carry with me into the world. That doctrine now guides my life and grounds me in my faith as well. As I age and mature, that doctrine develops from something I've created as an easy retrieval system to a deeper conviction and explanation as to why I am the way I am.

> "I'm not being a good steward of my relationship with my parents if I go to this party behind their backs. God says to honor my father and mother. I don't like it, but I respect it because there is value in it."

For a teen, that's probably as far as the thinking goes, although the conviction behind it is being reinforced.

For a young adult, as he or she begins to mature and continuing throughout his or her life, that thought process becomes more like this:

> "I'm not being a good steward of a relationship that calls me to respect the authority of my parents. God has placed them in authority over me, and I respect the authority of God. I need to humble myself and remember that God has given me boundaries in my life because He loves me and understands the dangers I face better than any earthly person ever could."

Don't underestimate your kids. I know some of you reading this are thinking, "Yeah, right. You can't reason with kids. They're going to do whatever they want to do." Sure, I'll concede that there are always those few who are more contrary than others, but with overwhelming confidence I say, "Show them the value in what God's Word says, and then never doubt them."

I once worked for a woman who had four kids very close in age. By the time I knew them, they were all in high school: a freshman, a sophomore, a junior, and a senior.

One of her daughters played the piano beautifully, and when I complimented her, she said, "You should hear my siblings."

Sometime after that, I asked her mom, "All of your kids play the piano? Wasn't that exhausting, trying to get them all to rehearsals and practice every day?"

I'll never forget her answer. She said, "It was hectic and very demanding on me, but if one did it, the others did too, because I never wanted any of them to feel that they weren't good enough at least to be given the opportunity to try."

And they all stuck with it. She has four accomplished pianists in her family.

Teach your teens well. Set the boundaries, and make sure they are clearly communicated so they understand why. Walk through the benefits and the consequences of every single thing, at the appropriate times, so it becomes second nature for them to think of their choices in such a way that they take ownership of them. We've all seen the impact of *Sesame Street* and *Dora the Explorer*: kids learn by repetition.

> "I always have a choice: if I make a good decision, ___ will happen. If I make a poor decision, ___ will happen."

Your family's mission statement will remind you all of your identity in Christ. It doesn't take the place of the Bible; it serves as a mental note that connects you to all you know the Bible to say and be. Even better, your children will grow up and carry this with them at every stage of their lives. It doesn't mean that they won't make mistakes; it means that they'll know how to get back on track when they do.

THE STANDARDS OF PROCEDURE

Finally, the standards of procedure. How do we execute the work?

> Upon opening the office at 7:30 a.m. sharp, the office

manager will first turn on the lights. The switch is located to the left of the front door. Next, the heat shall be set to 72 degrees, and the phone messages shall be documented and placed on the desk of the appropriate person.

The standards of procedure, or SOP, allow for continuity. Anyone can pick up where another has left off. This is fantastic, awesome news when used in conjunction with teaching biblical sexual integrity. By way of the SOP, parents can pick up where the pastors, youth directors, and teachers leave off, and vice versa. Mom and Dad tag team conversations with more ease because they've discussed their stance on things. The communion that God intended in His Church is ignited as the child's knowledge of God's love is deepened by respected people around him or her. In the years to come, God's incredible web of relationships is slowly exposed as that knowledge takes root, the child's faith matures, and his or her experiences expand.

The standards of procedure are also a really good place to start if you're trying to get comfortable talking to your kids about sex and relationships in the first place. The basics of dating are on everyone's minds from fifth grade up, so you have an automatic curiosity factor that acts in your benefit. Kids want to talk about dating, so start there and build on it.

Adults have a hard time talking to kids about sex. It's the ultimate act of bravery: having, or more likely showing, mental or moral strength to face a difficult situation. Fear or embarrassment of sharing their own dating stories and experiences, embarrassment of having to speak openly about sex with their kids, anxiety that they won't know what to say—trust me, it's not an easy subject to maneuver.

The fact that we hesitate to speak so openly about sex is a healthy sign of the innate regard we place on it. As adults, we know it's a big deal. We've seen its power and persuasions. We've also most likely experienced its awe as well. We do not want to mess this up for them. Embrace that! Don't shy away from it. Just as with everything else in life, the more acquainted you become with it, the easier it is to talk about it. Setting the standards of procedure for dating is very much like setting the standards of procedure for an organization. It allows everyone in the family to be on the same page and establishes the expectation to communicate with one another, parents to youth and youth to parents. "Hey, Mom, remember how you said I could date when I'm sixteen? Well, there's a girl I've got my eye on." To which Mom responds with something such as this to open up the dialogue: "Oh, really? What is she like? Tell me about her."

This is exactly the way to establish honest conversations and open the lines of communication when situations get more serious. If and when that happens, you'll have built a foundation with your teen from which to start. You will have some context and familiarity that, I promise, will make the uncomfortable talks much more successful.

When I'm speaking to a group of any size, I always like to make time at the end for the audience to ask questions. In a classroom, I might ask each student to write a question on a piece of paper and put it in a bucket; then I open the pieces of paper and talk about their questions together, but anonymously. I recommend doing this at home or with a youth group as well. Set up a topics of discussion bucket, and encourage your youth to ask anonymously any question on their mind.

Adults, try this out! Put a couple of questions in a jar every week, and your students will be so thankful for whoever opened the discussion for them. At home, parents can even write their responses on the paper and put it back in the bucket, if it's more comfortable to do it that way at first. Tell your kids that they can freely ask or tell you anything that's on their mind, and you'll check it every day. Don't get stuck there, though; feel it out, and when the climate begins to relax a little, start opening up to your kids. Talk about yourself, and relate your stories to their circumstances. Find a way to build a connection.

THE LINE IN THE SAND

If there is one question I get asked most often by teens, it is absolutely, without a doubt, THIS ONE:

"How far is too far?"

My response to that never changes:

"Why put yourself in that situation in the first place?"

When we entertain that question, we put ourselves in the awkward (and dangerous) state of questioning where to draw an acceptable line, pondering "how far is too far" in the midst of some very real temptation. At that point, then, we have to ask the next obvious question, "Acceptable to whom?"

To me?

To my date?

To my parents?

To my friends?

To God?

That way of thinking is subjective; it is based on opinions and emotions that change, rather than facts and logic that don't change.

How far is too far? Generally, the response I feel comfortable recommending is this: if you wouldn't do it in front of your parents, you shouldn't do it before your wedding night.

You see, dating relationships were never intended to include getting physical with the other person or seeing what amount of lust we could subject ourselves to. The purpose of dating is to find our future husband or wife, and only after marriage do we have the freedom to express our love through physical intimacy with that one person who is different from all the rest. Sadly, as a society, we've been taught to see this as the old-fashioned way rather than the intended way.

If I tried to sharpen my pencil in a food processor, I might destroy my food processor, but I would definitely destroy my pencil. That's because it was never intended to work that way. That's not old-fashioned; it's fact and reason.

Do you see how sexual marketing and propaganda have skewed our thinking? We often don't even realize how superficial our thinking has become until the truth is put before us and we're given the opportunity to compare and contrast.

This is truly where our standards of procedure come in.

We can face the pressures of society and our individual dating relationships by preparing for them first. Prior to battle, soldiers go through basic training. Prior to running a marathon, athletes train for it. And before nurses can work with the sick, they prepare in college and nursing school. Our relationships are the same way, and they are even more crucial than a profession or a pastime. This is our legacy we're talking about: our futures, our potential children's futures, and what we will impress on those we leave behind.

I'd say that's important enough for planning ahead.

I tell my teenagers this all the time: "Don't even put

yourselves in the position to be tempted. If you're mature enough to be contemplating sex, be mature enough to acknowledge that nothing good is going to come out of two young people being alone together."

Parents, this isn't about trusting your kids. This is about protecting your kids. You are protecting them from themselves, the sexual pressures they're facing all around them, their hormones, their maturing minds, and much more serious dangers such as sexual predators and drug-induced abuse. Your children deserve your safekeeping. That has nothing to do with trust and everything to do with diligence.

THE MOMENT OF TRUTH ABOUT TEMPTATION

We have always told our kids that we discipline them and set boundaries for them because we love them. If we didn't care about them, we wouldn't care what they did; however, we do care about them, so we completely care about what they do! The temptation to eat the apple in the Garden of Eden is the same temptation we are facing today. Consider the following temptations the world offers us:

- Abstinence until marriage is unrealistic

- You're old enough to make your own decisions about your life

- You don't need anyone else's approval

- It's okay as long as you're practicing safe sex

- Casual sex is totally normal

- It's okay to have sex with someone or move in together as long as you love each other

When those around us are saying these things, then we need to compare those statements with what our family (congregation or home) general operating system says.

In stark contrast to the world's direction, here are a few things we've always told our kids. Feel free to make them your own:

- Nonsense. We live in a culture of justification. Right is right, and wrong is wrong.

- You are free to make your own choices, but know that your poor choices have negative consequences. How will those consequences affect your future?

- You are smarter than the world gives you credit for. You are more capable than they give you credit for, and you are better than the world's expectations of you.

- Change the subject. Surround yourself with people who think like you do and share your mission statement. If the world insists on throwing casual, meaningless sex at you, just keep changing the subject. Change it back to things that are decent, honorable, and right.

We tell our children, "Why do all of these things matter? Because you are never alone, little one. You have Jesus Christ living in you."

Yes, I still call my teenagers little. They will forever be younger and more vulnerable than me in almost every way. Even when our bodies become frail, when our minds aren't as sharp as they once were, when our sons tower over us and our daughters outwit us, we are still the ones God chose, with great intention, to nurture and lead them. Sometimes we guide them in spite of our failings, and sometimes even by means of those same imperfections.

If I fill my body with the nutritious foods it needs to sustain me throughout my day and maintain an active lifestyle, I am less likely to struggle with obesity, anxiety, depression, feelings of uselessness, low self-confidence—all those nasty things. On the other hand, if I fill my body with momentary satisfactions that gratify me for just a little while, I will find myself craving those momentary satisfactions more and more. Like tacos. As my body is depleted of its stores of vitamins and nutrients, I will feel tired and cranky and sick. Now, I am free to do this to my body, of course, but such poor choices have negative consequences. Ironically, my freedom has led me into a prison within myself.

Approaching sex casually or not taking sex as seriously as it deserves does the same thing. When I discipline myself by choosing an apple over a donut, choosing healthy food that helps my whole body thrive over junk food that will make my body sick and tired, I exercise self-control and train myself to make good choices. In a similar way, when I treat sex seriously, I am disciplining my mind and body to exercise self-control. I am consciously defending myself against the allure of sexual immorality that will certainly surround me.

Teenagers and young adults want to have sex. If they don't yet, they will soon. Most teens have their first sexual encounter at their own home or the home of the other person. Unsupervised free time opens the way to temptation that can lead to poor choices. Even faithful Christian teens can make foolish choices in unsupervised environments. Teach them the value of their general operating system ahead of time so they don't have regrets later on. I always say, "Teenagers, talk about your thoughts and feelings with your parents and friends so that when you're contemplating what to do, you have accountability measures in place to get you through it.

Silence is a form of justification. Let me repeat myself: by remaining silent and keeping to yourself, you are separating yourself from the herd, and Satan will attack you. You were created to want this. Wanting to have sex makes you normal in every way. What's not normal and what you were not created for is having sex recklessly outside of marriage or with anyone except your husband or wife."

Keep your mission statement close in thought, word, and deed as a family and also as an individual.

> Frame your mission statement and hang it in a place where it's easily seen and recalled!

Directors of organizations sometimes have to make decisions without having their board of directors, or in our case, the family, present to help them. During those times, all they can do is fall back on what has already been established: their general operating system, made up of the Bible, the mission statement, and the standards of procedure.

Sometimes as the leader, you're also the parent. Sometimes you're the child or the pastor or the youth leader or the teacher. The beautiful thing about the family of God is that we mentor one another. We work in relationship with others in this great ebb and flow that always comes back to Jesus Christ, the source of all knowledge and understanding. He is the foundational block that allows us to build strong towers, remember? Through the working of the Holy Spirit, we are given wisdom and discernment to navigate through the temptations of the flesh so we can find peace in true love.

CHAPTER 6
Discussion Questions

» What standards do you have for the youth in your life? Are those standards clearly defined and understood?

» Why is confession and absolution an essential component of the family's general operating system?

» Craft a mission statement and standards of procedure for your family or the families with whom you work (for example, your congregation family).

CHAPTER 7

Starting Over

So you also must consider yourselves dead to sin and alive to God in Christ Jesus. Let not sin therefore reign in your mortal body, to make you obey its passions. Do not present your members to sin as instruments for unrighteousness, but present yourselves to God as those who have been brought from death to life, and your members to God as instruments for righteousness. For sin will have no dominion over you, since you are not under law but under grace.

ROMANS 6:11–14

My husband and I come from very different backgrounds. He chose to be abstinent all the way through college, until we got married when he was twenty-three years old. Even at that time, he was an oddity. How much more difficult is it today, twenty years later, for teens and young adults to hold on to their belief system? The choices that the kids in our lives make today will most certainly affect their future. That choice, or rather, all of those choices, are ultimately up to them. This is the most difficult part of parenting and shepherding youth, and it has been since the beginning of time. Adam and Eve certainly never intended or raised Cain to be a murderer. We do everything we can, with the help of God, to teach our children *diligently*, but at the end of the day, it is their choices, their decisions that determine their future. This realization makes us want to wrap them up in protective bubbles and lock them indoors, doesn't it? Allowing our kids to take ownership of their choices is the bravest thing we will ever do.

After I found out I was pregnant as a sophomore in college, I snapped out of it. I woke up. The consequences of my poor choices thus far were like a cold bucket of water in my face. I found myself looking for any justification I could find so that I didn't have to take the blame myself. I've learned, over the years, that I'm not unique in this way. It's always easier to cast the blame rather than accept it. Before I got pregnant with Bella, I felt empty and very alone in the world, even though I was surrounded by people.

I think that's one of the reasons God placed me in this line of work. He teaches me that my ministry is ultimately not about me helping them; rather, it's about Him helping us all through His Son and in relationship with one another.

It wasn't always easy for me to talk about sex, puberty, and relationships. Were you thinking that as soon as I learned I was pregnant, I set out to be the Sex Lady? Ha! Certainly not! I carried a lot of skeletons in my own closet and was in no hurry to expose them. But then God connected me with girls who reminded me how I used to feel, and I understood them. I recognized the same look in their faces, grasping at straws, that I had seen on my own.

In all my years of traveling and speaking, no one has

ever asked me why I got caught up in casual sex. However, people always ask me why I got pregnant at such a young age. That gives us a lot of insight into how we approach promiscuity at a societal level. Being unwed and pregnant was the side effect of a larger disease—sin. We all have the same root cause of sin: Satan, a fallen world, and a wicked flesh. Why do we constantly identify people by their sins, when the same root cause lies within each of us? "There's the pregnant girl." Or "There's that gay kid." When we identify people by their sins, it's like one cancer patient singling out another. Or in the words of Jesus, "Why do you see the speck that is in your brother's eye, but do not notice the log that is in your own eye?" (Matthew 7:3).

That's not to say that sex outside of marriage isn't sinful or that homosexuality isn't deserving of God's wrath, but it is to say that we are all sinful and we are all deserving of the same wrath. We are all broken and in need of healing.

Satan knows where we are vulnerable, and he attacks us when and where we are weak. My close relationships and support system were weak. I was so focused on being in control of my own life that all I cared about was myself and my priorities. My friends, on the other hand, were more grounded and focused. I remember admiring them for that. I admired their normal lives, but all the while, resentment was building within me, and I was growing more and more reckless and unpredictable. I felt strong and in control because I was on my own for the first time in my life. How ironic! That's precisely what Satan was using to target me. I had a total sense of security in myself and what I could do, and he knew it. I was like a deer standing in a field, oblivious to the hunter that was watching my every move.

To recap what I spoke of earlier—when we are alone, we are weak, but together, in community with others who carry the same operations manual as we do, we are unbreakable. There are so many of today's youth who are alone. They have parents who love them but are not present. Teenagers need relationship. They are watching us in order to figure out who they are and who they want to become. When we're not present, they're left to find that in someone else.

As a rule, I want to know my kids and my husband better than anyone has ever known them before. And I want them to know me the same way. The only way that's going to happen is by being together, a lot. As the mother, one of the most awesome gifts I have to give is that God made me the nurturer of the family. I get to be the one who is in charge of bringing us all together. Nothing makes me happier than to look around the room and see my family all in one place.

This urge tends to fluctuate in a lot of families, ours included; in the same way that we organize our menu of healthy meals so well for a month and then let it fall to the side for three, we find ourselves organizing family time and then letting it slide. This is a direct result of propaganda and consumerism in our modern culture. Fight it. We repent when we fail, and then we dive back in with the mind-set that this is a change in lifestyle, not an issue of better or-ganization. God does take into account our humanity and gives us grace upon grace to pull our families through it.

If you're reading this and are someone who loves teens but isn't a parent, you are the sunshine. The light of Christ in you makes you positively magnetic to these kids. I'm not sure if it's because of cultural marketing, the terminol-ogy they hear on social media, or because of the very keen vocabulary of evil, but so many youth use the exact same words to describe to me their feelings. They tell me that they're surrounded by darkness. They tell me that they're empty.

There is no greater joy in my life than the look in their eyes when I ask them what drives out darkness. What is the only thing in the world that drives away the dark? The Light.

In the glare of the cultural message of self-centeredness, the light of the Church may seem, at times, to be dimming. But that is Satan's lie, not God's truth. You are being used to open the eyes of the next generation to His mercies. Through your experiences, good and bad, the Holy Spirit turns that light into a laser beam and makes His presence known. He has placed you where you are for a reason—that you may do His will in the lives of His most vulnerable children—so just be yourself and allow God to use the gifts He's given you to make a connection, to build relationships. We all know that kids can see right through gimmicks. What they're craving is the love of the Father, and you might just be the bridge He's using to bring them to Himself.

My husband always says, "You are where you're supposed to be." If you are a father, a mother, a pastor, a teacher, a youth leader, or anything else that has placed you squarely in the middle of a situation involving teens, you are where you're supposed to be. You are ready. It's not by accident. In fact, it was very intentional. Share your stories. Through those stories, Christ will be revealed. Our two greatest human resources are our tongue and our testimony: a willingness to speak and an openness to share.

It's never too late for anyone to start over. That priest who botched the sex talk with his youth group; the father who disowned his homosexual son; the son who is struggling to find his identity in Christ. The teen who has bought into sex as a right rather than a gift, and the woman who is suffering after having an abortion. The young man with a sexually transmitted disease, and the teenage girl who is pregnant and alone. All our days were known to God; every word we'd ever speak, every act we'd ever commit, every failure and every sin. He knew it before a word was even on our lips (Psalm 139:4), and He deemed us worthy to create in spite of it all.

The point has never been about you being perfect.

It has always been about Jesus being perfect in your place and in mine.

How has the Potter refined each of us through the years? Don't we know better now than we did yesterday? or last week? or last year? Please don't get hung up on the things of the past. Repent and rest in the forgiveness you have in Jesus Christ at the end of every day. There is always, always hope in Him and in all that He is accomplishing in you to further His kingdom. You are His daily work of art, an all-original sculpture being made by God.

Paul says this in his Letter to the Church in Philippi:

> And I am sure of this, that He who began a good work in you will bring it to completion at the day of Jesus Christ. It is right for me to feel this way about you all, because I hold you in my heart, for you are all partakers with me of grace, both in my imprisonment and in the defense and confirmation of the gospel. For God is my witness, how I yearn for you all with the affection of Christ Jesus. And it is my prayer that your love may abound more and more, with knowledge and all discernment, so that you may approve what is excellent, and so be pure and blameless for the day of Christ, filled with the fruit of righteousness that comes through Jesus Christ, to the glory and praise of God. (Philippians 1:6–11)

CHAPTER 7

Discussion Questions

» What is the difference between viewing sex as a right and sex as a gift?

» In what areas do you consider yourself weak and therefore vulnerable to Satan's attacks? What can you do to strengthen these areas?

» How has God the Father refined you through the years? Give a specific example. Do you still find yourself judging people by their sins, even though we are all sinners ourselves?

» According to Paul, where is the source of righteousness?